THE COMPLETE BOOK OF

MICROWAVE BAKING

MARTY KLINZMAN · SHIRLEY GUY

PHOTOGRAPHY
PETER BROOKS

ACKNOWLEDGEMENTS

Our thanks to all those who so kindly supplied the accessories
used in the photographs, in particular to EM*ESS,
suppliers of quality china and silverware,
Grand and Grotty for the use of their china,
and Biggie Best for the printed fabrics.
We are also indebted to the following manufacturers
for the use of their products: Kenwood Home Appliances for their
electrical appliances and microwave ovens, Tedelex for their Brother
microwave ovens, Barlows for their National microwave ovens,
Sharp for their microwave ovens, Snowflake, Ruto Mills, and Tupperware.
To Gail Milella, a special thank you
for all the hours you spent testing recipes.

New Holland (Publishers) Ltd
37 Connaught Street
London W2 2AZ
United Kingdom

First published in 1989

Design and illustrations by Jennie Hoare
Edited by Linda de Villiers

Photosetting by Hirt and Carter
Typeface Novarese ITC Book 9.5 pt
Reproduction by Adcolour
Printed and bound by CTP Printers

ISBN 1 85368 060 5

CONTENTS

GOOD BAKING has always been considered an art with a lot of patience, skill and time involved. Most people love baked goods such as cakes, biscuits, puddings and desserts, and most of us enjoy baking – when we have the time.

By making use of your microwave oven, you can now bake all the family favourites and a host of delicious goodies for friends. In this book, we have strived to present great recipes and time-saving tips to make your microwave baking a success. We've gathered our best recipes for microwave cakes, desserts, breads, biscuits and baked savoury dishes, and tested them to please you.

Microwave baking is not difficult. Many of the principles of microwave baking are exactly the same as for conventional baking, but results are almost instant. So, if you want to skimp on preparation time but not on flavour, these microwave baking recipes are for you. With the recipes given here, you will produce good old-fashioned flavour with modern efficiency and speed.

HOW TO USE THIS BOOK

VARIABLE POWER LEVELS

All the recipes in this book have been tested using microwave ovens with variable power levels.

Each power level serves a definite purpose, so the recommended levels and settings should be used where possible. The power levels used in this book are as follows:

100% This is full power and is used to cook foods at a high temperature for a short time.

70% This level is used for foods that require more attention than those cooked at 100%.

50% This is often referred to as 'Medium' and is used for foods that need slower or more delicate cooking.

30% This level is used to defrost foods, but also to cook delicate items.

15% A low setting that is usually for softening cold foods or keeping food warm.

Some microwave ovens have a wider variety of power settings to give greater flexibility in cooking a wide range of foods.

NOTE Check the instruction book of your microwave oven for levels that correspond to the above.

COMBINATION COOKING

The recipes for combination microwave and convection cooking have been tested in several brands of microwave oven, including the popular Brother which is available in most countries. The instructions for baking in these ovens differ from manufacturer to manufacturer, and from model to model, each having its own power levels and programs for combination cooking. In recipes using combination/microwave energy, we have given the suggested program for the Brother as an example. At the end of each such recipe there is a program setting for this combination oven. No model numbers are given as these change from time to time. A reasonable cooking time range has been included in each program as some of the older models may require longer cooking times than the new improved models. Please check food at the minimum time given and add more time if necessary. Below is an example of the wording of the baking instructions for recipes using combination cooking:

BROTHER
Hi-Speed at 200 °C for 15-18 minutes.

NOTE As manufacturers update models of convection/microwave ovens constantly, the programs given for baking are to be used as a guide only. Please refer to the instruction manual for your microwave oven for similar recipes. This will ensure accurate programming and timing.

The great advantage of baking with a convection/microwave oven is that the food not only cooks quickly but also browns during cooking to give the traditional appearance. A number of recipes have been included here for use in combination ovens. For help with converting other recipes to combination cooking, find a similar recipe in your instruction book and use it as a guide for baking.

PRINCIPLES OF MICROWAVE BAKING

The use of ingredients and the methods of mixing them are the same for conventional and microwave baking, although the quantities of some of the ingredients and the cooking times are altered to suit microwave energy.

The cooking times given in each recipe are intended as a guide as several factors affect the exact timing of each recipe. Check at the minimum time given.

Always read each recipe through before starting to work. It is also a good idea to gather ingredients and equipment needed. Unless otherwise stated in the recipe, most ingredients should be at room temperature.

Follow the recipe carefully and measure accurately. A set of measuring utensils and good scales are essential basic items for baking. Baking recipes are developed to specific formulae and if these are followed exactly, successful cakes, breads and puddings will be the result. You may find it useful to look at the Art of Baking on page 82 before you start.

The biggest difference between conventionally baked foods and those baked in the microwave oven is that microwaved baked items do not brown. As many of the baked items are topped with icing, sauces or toppings, however, they will still look appetizing when served.

If baked food has become hard or dry, overcooking is indicated, so adjust the timing accordingly. If cooked food has hard or dry patches, the ingredients may not have been mixed properly, or the oven may have hot spots. Be sure to mix ingredients thoroughly during preparation and, if necessary, turn the pan during baking.

MICROWAVE TECHNIQUES

Many good cooks have hesitated to use the microwave oven for baking. Perhaps there has been a belief that the microwave could not bake successfully, or that there were new and difficult techniques to be learned. The recipes in this book will convince you that microwave baking is successful, and quick and easy too. Many of the basic techniques of baking still apply to microwave baking, so it is not necessary to learn a completely different method of preparation. Here are several points to consider when baking in the microwave oven.

ARRANGING FOOD When baking a number of small items such as American muffins or cup cakes, the best results are obtained when they are arranged in a circle on the turntable or microwave tray. It is best to leave the centre empty, as one small cake placed in the middle will take longer to bake than those on the outer edge, and may bake unevenly. Many large cakes and quick breads will bake more evenly if elevated on a microwave rack in the microwave oven.

* on microwave is 850 watts ?

TURNING Turning food in the microwave oven helps to ensure that it will cook evenly. Even microwave ovens with turntables may have hot or cold spots, so if you notice that cakes, puddings or breads cook unevenly, give the dish a quarter turn once or twice during baking.

SHIELDING Sensitive areas of some foods should be shielded from microwaves so that they do not overcook. As microwaves do not pass through metal, small pieces of aluminium foil can be used on the corners of square and rectangular dishes to prevent overcooking during microwave baking. Cut foil into triangular pieces and fold them over the edges of a square or rectangular dish when baking cakes, bars or desserts.

COOKING TIMES The cooking times given for all recipes in this book are intended as a guide, since the amount of microwave energy required will differ according to the make of oven used, the size and type of container, and the exact wattage of the oven. The time indicated above each recipe is a *guide* to the length of microwaving time and NOT the total preparation time.

STANDING TIME Microwaved foods continue to cook for a short period of time after being removed from the oven. Take this into consideration when baking in the microwave and remove cakes or puddings when they are still slightly moist on top. The standing time will complete the cooking.

COVERING Unless directed otherwise, do not cover food during baking as most baked foods do not require moist cooking.

TEXTURE There will be some difference in the texture of foods baked in the microwave oven because of the very quick cooking. Light mixtures such as sponge cakes will cook much more quickly than heavy mixtures such as fruit cakes, because the microwaves can penetrate a light mixture more easily than a heavy one.

QUANTITY The quantity of food in the microwave oven affects the cooking time. As the amount of food increases, so does the time needed to cook the food. If a recipe is doubled or halved, the cooking time will need to be adjusted accordingly. Best results are obtained with the quantities given in each recipe.

TEMPERATURE OF FOOD The temperature of the food placed in the microwave oven will affect the cooking time. If the food is taken from the refrigerator, the cooking time will be longer than for items that are at room temperature.

ADAPTING RECIPE TIMES The recipes in this book have been tested in microwave ovens with an output of 600-700 watts. Household current can vary during periods of peak use, such as early evening or in very cold weather. As a general rule, if you have a 500 watt microwave oven, add approximately 15-20 seconds to each minute of the cooking time.

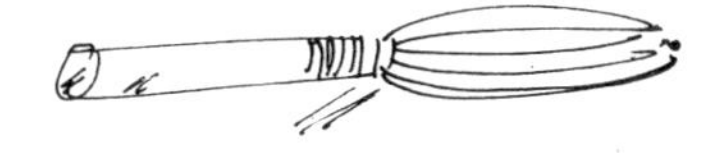

EQUIPMENT FOR MICROWAVE BAKING

A wide variety of containers can be used for microwave baking. There are special microwave plastic and glass containers available that will make baking easy. The sizes of many of these special containers correspond to the sizes of metal baking tins, so it is a good idea to investigate the shelves of your supermarket or discount store for microwave baking equipment.

☐ Most baked goods will rise higher in the microwave oven than in a conventional oven, so be sure to include some deep dishes in your selection.

☐ A large, deep ring dish is almost essential if you intend baking cakes and quick breads in the microwave oven as it allows the microwaves to penetrate from the centre as well as from the outside. It is possible to convert an ovenproof glass casserole to a ring dish by standing a glass tumbler, open side up, in the centre. Remember to grease the tumbler as well as the dish before adding the cake mixture.

☐ Remember that microwaves pass through glass, ceramic, plastic, pottery and paper.

☐ When baking by microwave energy alone, do not use metal baking tins, as the microwaves do not pass through them.

☐ Ovenproof glass containers, such as casseroles or flan dishes and pie plates can be used for microwave baking if the sizes correspond to sizes called for in the recipes.

☐ Straight-sided casseroles or soufflé dishes can also be used for cakes or puddings.

☐ A square baking dish can be used but the corners will need to be shielded with aluminium foil to prevent overcooking.

☐ Glass jugs and deep bowls are useful for making sauces, melting chocolate or heating liquids to be used in baking.

☐ A microwave oven rack is handy for elevating baking dishes to allow good circulation of the microwaves for more even baking.

☐ Individual paper containers for cup cakes, American muffins and small cakes can be used if you don't have a microwave muffin pan.

NOTE Metal baking tins can be used in some combinations microwave/convection ovens so check with the instruction book of the model you have, for exact details as to use and placement.

SAVOURIES

Ricotta Cashew Crêpes

SAVOURY DISHES stimulate the appetite and make tasty snacks with drinks, exciting starters for dinner parties, and delicious light lunches, as well as providing a welcome change from cakes and biscuits. Microwave baking is quick and easy, which means many traditional savoury dishes such as baked potatoes, quiches and pies, that used to be time-consuming to make, are now speedily produced at the touch of a button. Your microwave oven is also ideal for heating up fillings for crêpes and pitta bread. A combination microwave oven gives a crispy brown finish to choux or puff pastry, so there is no reason to shy away from these baked savouries.

SAVOURY SALMON RING

100%... 10 minutes
Serves 6

200 g (7 oz) canned pink salmon plus liquid
400 g (14 oz) canned cream of celery soup
125 g (4 oz) dry breadcrumbs
2 eggs
15 ml (1 tbsp) lemon juice
10 ml (2 tsp) chopped fresh dill or 2.5 ml (½ tsp) dried
SAUCE
200 g (7 oz) canned cream of celery soup
90 ml (3 fl oz) soured cream
60 ml (4 tbsp) dry white wine
10 ml (2 tsp) chopped fresh dill or 2.5 ml (½ tsp) dried

Combine salmon and liquid, celery soup and breadcrumbs. Beat eggs with lemon juice and dill and add to salmon mixture. Turn into a glass baking ring and cover with waxed paper. Microwave on 100% for 6-8 minutes, or until set. Stand for 8-10 minutes before turning out onto a serving plate.

For the sauce, combine ingredients and microwave for 2 minutes or until heated through.

BABY POTATOES WITH CAVIAR

100%... 14 minutes
Makes 12-20

500 g (18 oz) baby potatoes
200 ml (6½ fl oz) natural yoghurt
10 ml (2 tsp) lemon juice
salt and pepper to taste
5 ml (1 tsp) finely chopped fresh mint
60 g (2 oz) caviar or lumpfish roe
strips of lemon rind and parsley to garnish

Wash potatoes and pat dry. Prick skins well and arrange in a circular pattern in the microwave. Microwave on 100% for 10-14 minutes, or until baked, rearranging the potatoes halfway during the baking. Remove from the oven and cool.

Meanwhile make the filling. Mix yoghurt with lemon juice, salt and pepper and mint and chill. When potatoes are cold, slice off the tops and scoop out insides with a melon baller. Spoon filling into each one and top with a little caviar or lumpfish roe. Garnish with lemon rind and parsley. Serve chilled.

RICOTTA CASHEW CRÊPES

100%... 7 minutes
Serves 4

1 recipe wholemeal crêpes, cooked (page 93)
300 g (11 oz) fresh spinach, washed and trimmed
125 g (4 oz) ricotta cheese
60 g (2 oz) cashew nuts, chopped
2 egg yolks
2.5 ml (½ tsp) dried basil
45 ml (3 tbsp) chopped onion
60 ml (4 tbsp) single cream
salt and black pepper to taste
pinch of ground nutmeg
125 ml (4 fl oz) single cream
45 g (1½ oz) butter
60 g (2 oz) Cheddar cheese, grated

Blanch the spinach and drain well. Chop in a food processor. Add ricotta, nuts, egg yolks, basil, onion, 60 ml (4 tbsp) cream and seasonings. Mix well. Divide the mixture among the pancakes and roll up each one, placing in a greased casserole. Drizzle 125 ml (4 fl oz) cream over the top and microwave on 100% for 5-7 minutes. Dot with the butter and sprinkle grated cheese over the top. Brown under a grill and serve hot.

NEW POTATOES WITH MUSHROOMS & BACON

100%... 22 minutes
Makes 12-20

600 g (1 lb 5 oz) small new potatoes
30 g (1 oz) butter
1 small onion, finely chopped
1 garlic clove, finely chopped
150 g (5 oz) mushrooms, finely chopped
30 ml (2 tbsp) dry white wine
30 ml (2 tbsp) single cream
5 ml (1 tsp) chopped fresh dill or 2.5 ml (½ tsp) dried
salt and lemon pepper to taste
250 g (9 oz) streaky bacon rashers, rinds removed

Wash potatoes and pat dry. Prick skins well and place in a circular pattern on the turntable or microwave tray. Microwave on 100% for 10-14 minutes, or until baked, rearranging potatoes halfway through the cooking period. Cool potatoes while making the filling.

Place butter, onion and garlic in a microwave bowl and microwave for 2 minutes. Stir, add mushrooms and wine and microwave for a further 2 minutes. Mix well and drain off excess liquid. Add cream, dill and seasoning and stand until cool. When potatoes are cool, scoop out flesh with a small melon baller to form a small cavity and fill with the filling. Cut bacon rashers in half and stretch each rasher with the back of a knife, then wrap one around each of the potatoes, securing with a toothpick. Place half the potatoes in a circular pattern on a pie plate and microwave on 100% for 2 minutes to crisp the bacon. Remove and keep warm. Repeat with remaining potatoes. Serve warm.

SPINACH & RICOTTA PIE

100%, 70%, 50%... 13 minutes
Serves 4-6

300 g (11 oz) fresh spinach
1 onion, chopped
2 eggs
350 g (12 oz) ricotta cheese
salt and black pepper to taste
generous pinch of ground nutmeg
10 ml (2 tsp) plain flour
100 g (3½ oz) mushrooms, sliced
generous pinch of paprika
10 ml (2 tsp) dried breadcrumbs
10 ml (2 tsp) chopped fresh parsley
10 ml (2 tsp) chopped fresh mint

Place washed spinach leaves with the water that clings to the leaves into a bowl, add onion. Cover with vented plastic wrap and microwave on 100% for 4 minutes. Drain and chop coarsely. In another bowl, lightly beat the eggs, ricotta cheese, seasonings and flour. Stir in the mushrooms and the spinach. Turn into a lightly greased or sprayed 23-cm (9-in) pie plate. Combine remaining ingredients and sprinkle on the top. Microwave on 70% for 4 minutes and on 50% for 5 minutes.

SMOKED TROUT CUSTARDS

30%...20 minutes
Serves 6

175 g (6 oz) smoked trout
2 eggs
250 ml (8 fl oz) single cream
black pepper to taste
5-10 ml (1-2 tsp) lemon juice
5 ml (1 tsp) chopped fresh dill or
2.5 ml (½ tsp) dried
60 g (2 oz) Emmenthal cheese, grated
red lumpfish roe (optional)
fresh dill or parsley and lemon slices
to garnish

Place trout, eggs, cream, pepper, lemon juice and dill in a liquidizer and blend until smooth. Pour into 4 ovenproof ramekins and microwave on 30% for 15-20 minutes, or until just set. If mixture starts to bubble around the edges, turn off the oven for a few minutes, then continue cooking at 30%. Sprinkle with the cheese and melt under a grill. Garnish as shown and serve with toast fingers or Melba toast.

CHEESE STRAWS

100%...2 minutes
Makes about 30

125 g (4 oz) plain flour
2.5 ml (½ tsp) salt
5 ml (1 tsp) baking powder
pinch of cayenne
60 g (2 oz) margarine
45 ml (3 tbsp) grated Parmesan cheese
45 ml (3 tbsp) finely grated Cheddar
about 25 ml (5 tsp) water
30 ml (2 tbsp) toasted sesame
seeds (page 93)
paprika

Sift the dry ingredients into a bowl, add margarine and rub in. Add cheeses and mix lightly. Add water and work to a firm dough. Roll pastry to about 5-mm (¼-in) thickness. Sprinkle with sesame seeds and lightly roll seeds into pastry using a rolling pin and a piece of waxed paper. Sprinkle with paprika. Cut pastry into 6 × 1-cm (2¼ × ½-in) strips. Arrange strips on a plate or microwave dish, cook on 100% for 2 minutes.

BAKED STUFFED AVOCADOS

100%...8 minutes
Serves 4

100 g (3½ oz) canned pink salmon,
drained
½ small onion, chopped
60 g (2 oz) fresh breadcrumbs
2 ripe avocados
15 ml (1 tbsp) lemon juice
salt and black pepper to taste
60 g (2 oz) Cheddar cheese, grated
15 ml (1 tbsp) grated Parmesan cheese
paprika

Mash salmon and mix with chopped onion and breadcrumbs. Cut avocados in half and scoop out the flesh. Mix with lemon juice and mash well. Season to taste. Add to salmon and mix well. Mix in half the Cheddar cheese. Spoon mixture into the shells. Combine remaining Cheddar cheese, Parmesan and paprika, sprinkle liberally onto the filling. Arrange on a large plate with narrow ends of avocados towards the centre. Microwave on 100% for 6-8 minutes.

Smoked Trout Custards

Salmon & Dill Pinwheels

SALMON & DILL PINWHEELS

100%...2 minutes
plus Combination baking
Serves 8 or 9

125 g (4 oz) plain flour
125 g (4 oz) wholemeal flour
2.5 ml (½ tsp) salt
15 ml (1 tbsp) baking powder
10 ml (2 tsp) chopped fresh dill or
2.5 ml (½ tsp) dried
125 g (4 oz) butter or margarine
60 g (2 oz) Cheddar cheese, grated
150 ml (5 fl oz) milk
1 egg, beaten

FILLING
1 egg
30 ml (2 tbsp) chopped spring onion
30 ml (2 tbsp) chopped fresh parsley
15 ml (1tbsp) lemon juice
2.5 ml (½ tsp) salt
black pepper to taste
200 g (7 oz) canned pink salmon, drained

SAUCE
125 ml (4 fl oz) soured cream
60 ml (4 tbsp) milk
60 ml (4 tbsp) mayonnaise
15 ml (1 tbsp) chopped spring onion
10 ml (2 tsp) chopped fresh dill or
2.5 ml (½ tsp) dried
salt and pepper to taste

Combine flours, salt, baking powder and dill and mix well. Rub in the butter and stir in grated cheese. Combine milk and egg and add enough to the dry ingredients to form a dough. Turn out on a lightly floured surface and knead gently. Roll into a 32 × 36-cm (13 × 15-in) rectangle.

For the filling, combine all ingredients and mix well. Spread the mixture evenly over the dough and roll up Swiss roll fashion. Cut into 8 or 9 slices and place, cut-side down, in a circular pattern, in a greased 23-cm (9-in) baking dish. Bake according to instruction below. Remove from oven and allow to stand while making the sauce.

Combine all ingredients for the sauce and microwave on 100% for 2 minutes, or until heated through.

To serve, place one pinwheel roll on each plate and top with sauce. Garnish with spring onion and dill.

BROTHER
Hi-Speed at 200°C for 7-12 minutes.

CREAM CHEESE & CAVIAR BLINIS

70%...5 minutes
Makes 18

Lumpfish roe is recommended as substitute for real caviar!

250 g (9 oz) cream cheese
30 ml (2 tbsp) single cream
1 egg
10 ml (2 tsp) plain flour
salt and black pepper
15 ml (1 tbsp) snipped chives
125 g (4 oz) red or black lumpfish roe
18 small thick crêpes (page 93)
about 30 ml (1 oz) butter
250 ml (8 fl oz) soured cream
paprika

Combine the cream cheese, cream, egg, flour, seasonings and chives. Place lumpfish roe in a colander, rinse well with cold water and allow to drain. This will prevent discoloration. Place a small spoonful of the cheese mixture on one side of each crêpe, top with a spoonful of lumpfish roe, now roll up or fold into four. Place in a shallow dish, dot with butter and cover with vented plastic wrap. Microwave on 70% for about 5 minutes, until piping hot. Serve with soured cream sprinkled with paprika.

Cream Cheese & Caviar Blinis

HOT TUNA SALAD PITTAS

100%...21 minutes
Serves 4

4 pitta breads (page 23)
200 g (7 oz) canned tuna in oil
cooked rice
1 bunch spring onions, sliced
30 ml (2 tbsp) chopped red
or green pepper
45 ml (3 tbsp) sliced celery
30 g (1 oz) butter or margarine
1 large tomato, skinned and chopped
100 ml (3½ fl oz) mayonnaise
15 ml (1 tbsp) lemon juice
2.5 ml (½ tsp) mixed herbs
salt and black pepper to taste

Cut each pitta bread in half and open to form pockets. Drain the tuna, flake and mix with the rice. Microwave the onion, red or green pepper and celery with the butter on 100% for 3-4 minutes, stirring twice. Add the tomato and microwave for 1 minute more. Add mixture to the tuna and rice. Stir in mayonnaise, lemon juice, herbs and season well with salt and pepper. Spoon mixture into pittas and place 2 halves at a time, on a plate. Microwave for 2-4 minutes, or until heated through. Keep warm and repeat with the remaining pittas. Serve with a green salad.

PICNIC LOAF

70%...26 minutes
Serves 6-8

1 round loaf of bread, unsliced
100 ml (3½ fl oz) milk
45 ml (3 tbsp) chopped fresh parsley
1 small tomato, peeled and chopped
2 eggs
7.5 ml (1½ tsp) salt
pepper to taste
2.5 ml (½ tsp) dried oregano
2.5 ml (½ tsp) dried basil
500 g (18 oz) lean minced beef
250 g (9 oz) lean minced veal
45 ml (3 tbsp) grated cheese
30 ml (2 tbsp) finely chopped onion

Slice a small lid from the top of the bread. Pull out enough soft bread from the centre of the loaf to leave a 1-cm (½-in) shell. Crumb the bread and place 60 g (2 oz) in a large mixing bowl. Stir in milk and chopped parsley. Add all remaining ingredients to the bread mixture and combine well. Pack the mixture into the bread shell and replace the lid. Place loaf in a roasting bag and wrap tightly. Make 2 or 3 slits in the bag near the top. Place loaf in a dish and microwave on 70% for 22-26 minutes. If using a temperature probe, internal temperature should be 57 °C. Remove loaf from oven and stand for at least 10 minutes before serving. To serve, cut in wedges and serve with mustard or tomato sauce. To serve cold, stand for 20 minutes to cool (do not unwrap), then refrigerate until needed.

CHEESE & HAM GOUGÈRE

100%...11 minutes
plus Convection and
Combination baking
Serves 4

PASTRY
150 ml (5 fl oz) water
45 g (1½ oz) butter or margarine
60 g (2 oz) plain flour
generous pinch of salt
2 eggs
75 g (2½ oz) Emmenthal cheese,
grated

FILLING
30 g (1 oz) butter
100 g (3½ oz) mushrooms, sliced
60 ml (4 tbsp) finely chopped onion
30 ml (2 tbsp) plain flour
30 ml (2 tbsp) dry sherry
125 ml (4 fl oz) chicken stock
125 ml (4 fl oz) single cream
5 ml (1 tsp) Dijon mustard
200 g (7 oz) cooked ham, chopped
15 ml (1 tbsp) chopped fresh parsley
30 ml (2 tbsp) seasoned tomato sauce,
not ketchup
60 g (2 oz) Cheddar cheese, grated
2.5 ml (½ tsp) dried oregano
1 tomato, sliced

To make the pastry, place water and butter in a deep microwave bowl and microwave on 100% for 3-4 minutes, or until boiling and butter has melted. Remove from oven and add flour and salt all at once. Beat to a smooth ball, then leave till lukewarm.

Add eggs, one at a time, beating after each. Be careful not to add too much egg, the mixture should still hold its shape. Mix in grated cheese. Spoon mixture around the sides of a round or oval, well-greased baking dish.

To make the filling, microwave butter for 45 seconds to melt. Add mushrooms and onion and microwave for 3 minutes. Stir in flour, then gradually mix in sherry, chicken stock, cream and mustard. Microwave for 3 minutes, stirring every minute, then add ham, parsley, tomato sauce, cheese and oregano. Mix well and place in the centre of the pastry.

Bake at 220 °C (425 °F) in a pre-heated convection oven for 20 minutes. Top with sliced tomato and continue baking according to instructions below. Garnish with fresh parsley if desired.

BROTHER
Hi-Speed at 180 °C for 10-13 minutes.

CHEESE RAMEKINS

70%...5 minutes
Serves 4

4 eggs
125 ml (4 fl oz) single cream
125 g (4 oz) Cheddar cheese, grated
salt and black pepper
5 ml (1 tsp) snipped chives
15 g (½ oz) butter

Mix eggs, cream, cheese, salt and pepper and chives. Use the butter to grease four ramekins or individual custard dishes. Divide the egg mixture among the dishes and microwave on 70% for 4-5 minutes. The sides should be soft and the centres soft and creamy.

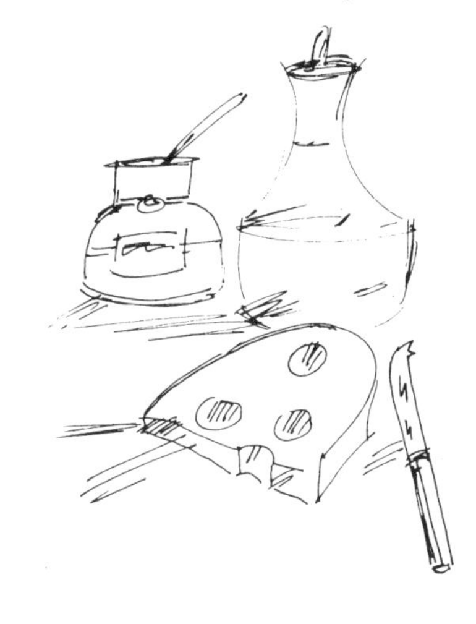

BRIE WITH ALMONDS & BUTTER

100%, 70%...5 minutes
Serves 6-8

150 g (5 oz) Brie cheese
30 g (1 oz) unsalted butter
30 ml (2 tbsp) flaked almonds

Place cheese on a microwave-proof serving plate. Combine butter and almonds in a bowl and microwave on 100% for 3-4 minutes, or until almonds are toasted. Spoon almond mixture over Brie and microwave on 70% for about 1 minute, or until cheese is heated through. Serve as a spread with savoury biscuits or Melba toast.

CHEESY BACON STICKS

100%...12 minutes
Makes 20

10 streaky bacon rashers, rinds removed
45g (1½ oz) grated Parmesan cheese
20 grissini (Italian breadsticks)

Cut bacon rashers in half lengthways. Sprinkle bacon with cheese, and press onto bacon. Wrap one strip in a spiral around each breadstick. Place waxed paper on each of three paper plates, divide breadsticks among plates. Cover with waxed paper. Microwave each plate on 100% for 3-4 minutes, or until bacon is cooked.

Brie With Almonds & Butter

ONION & MUSHROOM QUICHES

100%, 70%, 50%...17 minutes
Serves 6

200 g (7 oz) shortcrust pastry (page 87)
30 g (1 oz) butter
1 onion, chopped
200 g (7 oz) fresh mushrooms, sliced
30 ml (2 tbsp) finely chopped green pepper
45 ml (3 tbsp) plain flour
125 ml (4 fl oz) milk
2 eggs, beaten
90 ml (3 fl oz) single cream
salt and black pepper to taste
15 ml (1 tbsp) chopped fresh parsley
5 ml (1 tsp) chopped fresh oregano

Roll out pastry dough and cut circles to fit a microwave muffin pan. Prick pastry all over with a fork. Microwave on 70% for 4-5 minutes, pushing pastry back into the cups if necessary.

To make the filling, microwave butter in a large bowl on 100% for 45 seconds. Add onion, mushrooms and green pepper. Microwave for 2 minutes. Stir in flour and gradually stir in milk. Microwave on 70% for 1-2 minutes, stirring twice. Mix a little of the hot mixture into the beaten eggs, then return to the bowl, mixing well. Add remaining ingredients and onion mixture. Spoon into the pastry shells. Microwave on 50% for 5-7 minutes, or until a knife inserted near the centre comes out clean. Stand for 3-4 minutes before serving.

SPICY BAKED PECANS

100%...9 minutes
Makes about 300 g (11 oz)

60 g (2 oz) butter
30 ml (2 tbsp) Worcestershire sauce
10 ml (2 tsp) soy sauce
5 ml (1 tsp) garlic salt
300 g (11 oz) pecan halves

Place butter, Worcestershire sauce, soy sauce and garlic salt in a casserole. Microwave on 100% for 1 minute. Add pecan halves, stir to coat well. Microwave for 6-8 minutes, stirring at least twice. Drain off any excess butter and turn onto paper towel. Store in an airtight container.

Onion & Mushroom Quiches

YEAST BAKING

Front left to right *Rye Bread & Plaited Egg Bread* Back left to right *Crusty Country Bread & Herb Cheese Swirl*

THE AROMA of yeast bread baking is enough to start the hunger pangs and conjures up images of butter melting on a freshly baked roll or slice of home-made bread. The microwave oven will prove yeast doughs, and bake breads quickly and without effort, but breads baked by microwave energy will not brown or form the characteristic golden crust we have come to expect. Combination baking, using convection and microwave energy, gives the traditional results, so in this chapter, you will find several recipes using this method.

CHEESE 'N HERB BROWN LOAF

100%, 50%... 14 minutes
Makes 1 × 18-cm (7-in) round loaf

250 g (9 oz) plain flour
250 g (9 oz) wholemeal flour
15 ml (1 tbsp) instant dried yeast
5 ml (1 tsp) salt
5 ml (1 tsp) mixed herbs
60 g (2 oz) butter
250 ml (8 fl oz) milk
15 g (½ oz) butter
30 ml (1 oz) finely chopped onion
90 g (3 oz) Cheddar cheese, grated
15 ml (1 tbsp) wheat germ
15 ml (1 tbsp) sesame seeds

Combine plain flour, wholemeal flour, yeast, salt and mixed herbs in a mixing bowl. Cut the 60 g (2 oz) butter into cubes and rub into the dry ingredients. Microwave milk in a jug on 100% for about 1 minute until blood heat, then add to dry ingredients. Mix to form a soft but not sticky dough. Place 15 g (½ oz) butter in a small jug, microwave for 15 seconds, add onion and microwave for 1 minute. Drain onion, reserving the butter. Knead dough until smooth and elastic, working in the chopped onion and two-thirds of the cheese.

Shape dough into a smooth ball and place in a well-greased deep, 18-cm (7-in) soufflé dish. Cover with paper towel and prove in the microwave oven by microwaving on 100% for 15 seconds, then allow to stand for 10 minutes. Repeat process at least once more until the dough has doubled in volume.

Brush with reserved melted butter and sprinkle with wheat germ, sesame seeds and remaining cheese.

Microwave on 50% for 6 minutes, then on 100% for 3-4 minutes. Gently remove the loaf from the dish, place on a paper towel in the microwave and microwave for 1 minute. Stand for 5 minutes, then cool on a wire rack.

CRUSTY COUNTRY BREAD

Combination baking
Makes 2 loaves

15 ml (1 tbsp) instant dried yeast
475 g (17 oz) bread flour
10 ml (2 tsp) salt
10 ml (2 tsp) sugar
about 375 ml (12 fl oz) warm water

Combine yeast, flour, salt and sugar in a large mixing bowl. Add enough warm water to make a firm dough. Knead until smooth and elastic, about 5 minutes by machine or 10 minutes by hand. Cover and let rise in a warm place, or prove according to microwave instructions until almost tripled in volume. Knock down and knead about 2 minutes. Cover and let rise again until doubled. Knock down, divide dough in half and shape to fit greased loaf pans or shape into rounds and place in large, greased soufflé dishes. Let rise again until doubled. Bake loaves separately as directed below until golden brown and hollow-sounding when tapped. Cool on wire racks.

BROTHER
Hi-Speed at 190 °C for 18-24 minutes.

MALTED FLOWER-POT LOAF

100%... 11 minutes
Serves 6-8

450 g (1 lb) wholegrain bread mix
15 g (½ oz) margarine
30 ml (2 tbsp) malt extract
300 ml (10 fl oz) water
60 ml (4 tbsp) crushed wheat

Place wholegrain bread mix in a large mixing bowl. Rub in the margarine. Place malt extract and water in a measuring jug, microwave on 100% for 1-1½ minutes until blood heat. Add liquid to flour mixture and knead with a dough hook for about 4 minutes. Place dough in a lightly oiled roasting bag, microwave on 100% for 15 seconds, rest 7 minutes, then repeat. Knead dough lightly and shape to fit a clay flower-pot, or use a small rectangular clay casserole. Roll the top of the dough in crushed wheat, pressing in firmly. Cover loosely with plastic wrap, microwave for

15 seconds, rest 5 minutes, and repeat twice more until the dough has doubled in volume. Remove plastic wrap. Microwave on 100% for 7-8 minutes. Cool for 10 minutes before serving.

PLAITED EGG BREAD

Combination baking
Makes 1 loaf

350 g (12 oz) plain flour
15 ml (1 tbsp) instant dried yeast
5 ml (1 tsp) salt
125 ml (4 fl oz) very warm water
2 large eggs
100 ml (3½ fl oz) oil
60 g (2 oz) sugar
30 g (1 oz) butter, softened
beaten egg for glazing
poppy or sesame seeds (optional)

Combine 125 g (4 oz) of the flour with yeast and salt in a large mixing bowl. Add warm water and mix to moisten, then beat for 3 minutes at medium speed. Combine eggs, oil, sugar and butter and beat well. Add to the yeast mixture and beat thoroughly. Add enough of the remaining flour to make a soft dough. Knead until smooth and elastic. Cover and let rise in a warm place until doubled in volume. Knock down and let rise again. Knock down and divide dough into 3 equal pieces. Roll each piece into a 30-cm (12-in) rope. Lay 3 ropes parallel and begin plaiting, working from the middle. Pinch the ends and turn them under to secure. Place loaf on a greased baking sheet. Cover and let rise until doubled. Brush with beaten egg and sprinkle with seeds if desired. Bake according to instructions below until golden and hollow-sounding when tapped. Cool on wire rack.

BROTHER
Hi-Speed at 190 °C for 18-26 minutes.

Honey Wheat Bread

Cheesy Bubble Loaf

HONEY WHEAT BREAD

100%...2 minutes
plus Combination baking
Makes 2 loaves

400 g (14 oz) wholemeal flour
15 ml (1 tbsp) salt
15 ml (1 tbsp) instant dried yeast
250 ml (8 fl oz) milk
125 g (4 oz) honey
30 g (1 oz) butter
250 ml (8 fl oz) warm water
150 g (5 oz) seedless raisins
175 g (6 oz) plain flour

Combine wholemeal flour, salt and yeast in a large mixing bowl. Microwave milk, honey and butter on 100% for 1-2 minutes, until milk is very warm. Add warm water to the milk mixture and add liquid to the dry flour mixture. Mix to moisten, then beat for 3 minutes at medium speed of an electric mixer. Stir in raisins, then mix in enough of the plain flour to form a stiff dough. Knead until smooth and elastic, about 12 minutes by hand or 5 minutes by machine. Cover and prove according to microwave instructions. Knock dough down and divide in half. Shape into loaves to fit two well-greased loaf pans or shape into two oval loaves and place on a greased baking sheet. Cover and let rise in a warm place or prove according to microwave instructions. Bake each loaf separately, as directed below until golden brown and hollow-sounding when tapped. Cool on wire racks.

BROTHER
Hi-Speed at 190 °C for 18-24 minutes.

HERB CHEESE SWIRL

Combination baking
Makes 1 loaf

45 g (1½ oz) softened butter
10 ml (2 tsp) oil
2.5 ml (½ tsp) each dried basil, tarragon, thyme and oregano
pinch of pepper
30 ml (2 tbsp) brown onion soup powder
15 ml (1 tbsp) instant dried yeast
600 g (1 lb 5 oz) plain flour
30 ml (2 tbsp) sugar
15 ml (1 tbsp) salt
500 ml (16 fl oz) very warm water
150 g (5 oz) Gruyère cheese, grated
1 egg white

Use the softened butter to grease a large, deep springform ring pan very well. Combine oil, herbs, pepper and brown onion soup powder, mixing well. Stand for at least 15 minutes. Place yeast, half the flour, the sugar and salt in the mixing bowl. Stir to combine. Add warm water to the yeast mixture, beating on low speed to moisten. Then mix on medium speed for 3 minutes. Mix in oil and herb mixture. Stir in enough of the remaining flour to make a soft dough. Knead until smooth and elastic, 10 minutes by hand or 4 minutes by machine. Cover and prove according to microwave instructions. Knock dough down and roll into a large circle. Sprinkle with grated cheese, bring the edges towards the centre forming a ball again. Let rest 8-10 minutes, then roll into a large rectangle. Roll up tightly, Swiss roll fashion, starting at the long edge. Pinch seam to seal. Join open ends to form a circle. Place in the prepared ring pan, seam-side down. Cover and let rise until doubled. Brush with egg white and snip surface of dough at 4-cm (1½-in) intervals with scissors. Bake as directed below, until golden brown and hollow-sounding when tapped. Turn out on a wire rack to cool.

BROTHER
Hi-Speed at 220 °C for 5 minutes, then at 190 °C for 18-24 minutes.

CHEESY BUBBLE LOAF

Combination baking
Makes 1 loaf

450 g (1 lb) plain flour
15 ml (1 tbsp) instant dried yeast
15 ml (1 tbsp) sugar
5 ml (1 tsp) salt
225 ml (7 fl oz) water
30 g (1 oz) butter
15 ml (1 tbsp) honey
2 large eggs
1 egg white
60 g (2 oz) Cheddar cheese, grated
2.5 ml (½ tsp) baking powder
beaten egg yolk
poppy seeds

Combine half the flour, the yeast, sugar and salt in a large mixing bowl. Combine water, butter and honey and heat to lukewarm. Add to the flour mixture and beat for 2 minutes on medium speed of an electric mixer. Beat in the eggs and egg white, mixing well. Stir in cheese. Add half the remaining flour and the baking powder and mix in. Add enough of the remaining flour to form a soft dough. Knead dough until smooth and elastic, about 10 minutes by hand or 4 minutes with an electric mixer. Prove according to microwave instructions. Knock down and let rise again until doubled. Knock down once more. Knead gently for about 2 minutes.

Divide dough into balls about the size of large walnuts. Layer balls of dough in a large greased soufflé dish, placing the last ball in the centre. Prove according to microwave instructions, then brush with beaten egg yolk and sprinkle with sesame seeds. Bake according to the instructions below until golden brown and hollow-sounding when tapped. Remove from the dish and allow to cool on a wire rack.

BROTHER
Hi-Speed at 190 °C for 18-22 minutes.

NOTE Be sure to check your instruction book for the use of trivets metal pans or racks in the convection oven.

WALNUT BREAD

100%...2 minutes
plus Combination baking
Makes 1 loaf

This bread goes well with cheese, chilled grapes and a white or rosé wine. Bake it in a combination oven.

475 g (17 oz) plain flour
60 g (2 oz) wholemeal flour
15 ml (1 tbsp) instant dried yeast
5 ml (1 tsp) salt
250 ml (8 fl oz) milk
75 ml (2½ fl oz) water
100 g (3½ oz) walnuts, coarsely chopped
125 g (4 oz) onion, finely chopped
125 g (4 oz) butter, softened

Combine half the plain flour, the wholemeal flour, yeast and salt in a large mixing bowl. Microwave milk and water on 100% for 1-2 minutes until very warm. Add to the dry ingredients and mix to moisten. Beat on medium speed for 3 minutes. Stir in the nuts, onion and butter and mix well. Blend in enough of the remaining flour to make a stiff dough. Cover and prove according to microwave directions. Knock dough down and knead for 2-3 minutes. Shape into a ball and place on a baking sheet. Let rise, uncovered, for about 15 minutes. Bake according to instructions below until loaf is nicely browned and sounds hollow when tapped. Cool on a wire rack.

Walnut Bread

BROTHER
Hi-Speed at 220 °C for 10 minutes, then bake on convection at 180 °C for about 25-30 minutes.

BREAD ROLLS

100%...12 minutes
Makes about 16-32

To make bread rolls, use a yeast recipe such as Honey Wheat Bread, Plaited Egg Bread, Seed Loaves, Walnut Bread or one of your own favourite recipes. Follow the recipe directions for mixing and the first proving of the dough. The number of rolls made will depend on the yield of the bread recipe. A one-loaf recipe will make about 16 rolls.

For a one-loaf recipe, grease two 20-cm (8-in) cake dishes. Divide dough into equal pieces (about 16) and shape each piece into a smooth ball. Place one ball in the centre of each prepared dish and place seven balls around the central ball. Cover and prove as directed for yeast loaves until doubled in volume. Uncover, brush with a little milk and sprinkle with poppy seeds, sesame seeds or savoury biscuit crumbs. Stand one dish at a time on a rack in the microwave oven and microwave on 100% for 4-6 minutes, or until well risen and firm to the touch. Stand in the dishes for 10 minutes, then turn out and leave to cool on a wire rack.

If desired, omit the seeds or crumbs and place under a hot grill for a few minutes after baking to brown the tops. Pull rolls apart to serve.

PITTA BREAD

100%...21 minutes
Makes 8

5 ml (1 tsp) each sugar and salt
5 ml (1 tsp) instant dried yeast
450 g (1 lb) plain flour
45 g (1½ oz) butter or margarine
250-275 ml (8-9 fl oz) warm water

Combine sugar, salt, yeast and flour. Rub butter into the flour mixture. Add the warm water all at once and mix to a dough. Knead until dough is smooth and elastic, about 10 minutes by hand or 4 minutes with an electric mixer. Place dough in an oiled bowl, turning to oil the dough. Cover loosely with plastic wrap and microwave for 15 seconds on 100%, then stand for 8-10 minutes. Repeat microwaving and standing once or twice more, or until dough has doubled in volume. Knock dough down, knead until smooth, then divide into 8 equal portions. On a floured board, roll each portion into a flat oval. Dust with flour and microwave, one at a time, on 100% for 1½ minutes. Turn pitta over and microwave 40-50 seconds more. Place on a wire rack to cool. Repeat with remaining pittas. To use, cut in half and open carefully to form pocket.

YEAST-BASED PIZZA

100%, 30%...24 minutes
Serves 4

125 ml (4 fl oz) warm water
5 ml (1 tsp) dried yeast
2.5 ml (½ tsp) sugar
250 g (9 oz) plain flour
2.5 ml (½ tsp) salt
30 ml (2 tbsp) oil
700 ml (22 fl oz) tomato topping (page 93)
400 g (14 oz) mozzarella cheese, thinly sliced
60 g (2 oz) canned anchovies

Combine the water, yeast and sugar in a small jug. Sprinkle 45 ml (3 tbsp) of measured flour onto the yeast mixture, do not stir in. Cover with plastic wrap. Microwave for 30 seconds on 100%. Set aside until bubbling. Sift remaining flour and salt into a mixing bowl. Add oil to the yeast mixture, then add to the flour. Mix to a firm dough, then knead until smooth. Shape into a ball, brush with a little extra oil. Place in a lightly greased roasting bag. Microwave for 10 seconds, rest for 10 minutes. Repeat twice more; until dough has doubled in size. Divide dough into four, knead each piece lightly. Roll each portion into a 20-cm (8-in) round. Grease 4 plates and dust lightly with flour. Cover plates with dough. Microwave each plate on 30% for 15 seconds, rest for 4 minutes. Repeat at least twice more, until dough has doubled in volume. Spread tomato topping over each pizza. Cover with slices of cheese and then with strips of anchovy. Microwave pizzas, one at a time on 100% for 5 minutes. Stand for 3 minutes before serving.

VARIATIONS

Seafood 200 g (7 oz) canned shrimps, 225 g (8 oz) canned mussels drained, 15 ml (1 tbsp) chopped parsley. Arrange on top of cheese.

Mushroom 300 g (11 oz) mushrooms, sliced, 30 ml (2 tbsp) oil, pinch of dried thyme. Combine ingredients and spoon on top of cheese.

Salami 20 thin slices salami. Arrange salami around the edges of the pizza on top of the cheese.

Tuna 200 g (7 oz) canned tuna, drained and flaked, 10 ml (2 tsp) lemon juice, 20 ml (4 tsp) chopped capers. 2.5 ml (½ tsp) thyme. Combine ingredients and spoon on top of cheese.

RYE BREAD

100%...7 minutes
Makes 1 loaf

10 ml (2 tsp) brown sugar
125 g (4 oz) bread flour
300 g (11 oz) rye flour
7.5 ml (1½ tsp) salt
15 ml (1 tbsp) instant dried yeast
350-375 ml (11-12 fl oz) warm water
oil
caraway seeds

Combine sugar, both flours and salt. Microwave for 20 seconds. Stir in yeast. Add enough of the warm water to make a soft dough. Knead until smooth and elastic. Oil a large bowl, place dough in the bowl, turning to oil the dough. Cover loosely with plastic wrap and microwave on 100% for 15 seconds. Allow to stand for 8-10 minutes, then repeat microwaving and standing twice more, or until dough has doubled in volume. Knock dough down, knead until smooth, then shape into a ball. Make a slash across the top of the dough with a sharp knife. Place dough in a large, round, greased dish. Brush with a little oil and sprinkle with caraway seeds. Cover loosely and prove as above until dough has doubled in volume. Remove plastic wrap. Microwave on 100% for 5-6 minutes. Allow to stand for 10 minutes, then turn out and cool on a wire rack.

AMERICAN MUFFIN LOAF

100%...16 minutes
Makes 2 loaves

500 ml (16 fl oz) milk
125 ml (4 fl oz) water
15 ml (1 tbsp) sugar
generous 30 g (1 oz) fresh yeast
600 g (1 lb 5 oz) plain flour
5 ml (1 tsp) salt
2.5 ml (½ tsp) bicarbonate of soda
cornmeal

Place milk and water in a jug, microwave on 100% for 1-1½ minutes until warm. Add sugar and yeast and stir until yeast is well combined. Sprinkle mixture with 30 ml (2 tbsp) of the measured flour and cover with vented plastic wrap. Microwave for 10 seconds on 100%, stand for 3 minutes and repeat once more. The top will begin to foam. Meanwhile sift remaining flour, salt and bicarbonate of soda into a large bowl. Pour in the yeast mixture and mix with an electric mixer for about 4 minutes. Grease two 25 × 12-cm (10 × 5-in) loaf pans and sprinkle a little cornmeal over the base and sides. Spoon in the bread mixture, dust tops with a little cornmeal. Cover with plastic wrap, microwave for 15 seconds, then rest for 10 minutes. Repeat 2-3 times until the bread has doubled in size. Microwave each loaf separately for 5½-6½ minutes. The surface of the cooked loaves will be pale in colour. Stand for 10 minutes before removing from the pan. To serve, slice and toast, serve with butter and honey or syrup.

RUM BABAS

100%... 20 minutes
Serves 8

150 ml (5 fl oz) milk
12.5 ml (2½ tsp) dried yeast
30 g (1 oz) caster sugar
250 g (9 oz) plain flour
pinch of salt
100 g (3½ oz) butter or margarine
2 eggs, lightly beaten
60 g (2 oz) currants, soaked in
30 ml (2 tbsp) rum
SYRUP
300 ml (10 fl oz) water
200 g (7 oz) sugar
60 ml (4 tbsp) dark rum
TO SERVE
90 g (3 oz) apricot jam
250 ml (8 fl oz) whipping cream, beaten

Pour milk into jug, microwave on 100% for about 15 seconds, until blood heat. Add yeast and 5 ml (1 tsp) sugar, stir to combine. Sprinkle 30 ml (2 tbsp) of the measured flour on top of milk, cover with plastic wrap. Microwave for 10 seconds, then stand 5 minutes. Repeat microwaving and standing once more. Sift remaining flour and salt into a food processor work bowl or a mixing bowl, add remaining sugar. Microwave butter for 30 seconds to soften. The butter should not be melted. Add very soft butter to eggs, beat lightly and stir in yeast mixture. Add to flour mixture and beat very well until a smooth soft batter forms. Stir in currants. Grease or spray 8 custard cups very well, turn batter into moulds and cover with plastic wrap.

To prove mixture, arrange in a circle in microwave. Microwave on 100% for 10 seconds, rest for 10 minutes, repeat microwaving and resting twice more. The mixture should rise to the top of the moulds. Remove plastic wrap and microwave for 4½-6 minutes, until just dry on top. Stand for 10 minutes before turning out onto a wire rack.

For the syrup, combine water and sugar in a jug and microwave for 10 minutes, stirring after 5 minutes. Cool slightly and add rum. Place a plate under the warm babas, spoon syrup over until it is completely absorbed. Transfer to a serving plate and chill. Microwave jam for 1-2 minutes until warm. Brush top and sides with jam. Decorate with swirls of cream.

Kugelhopf

KUGELHOPF

100%... 12 minutes
Makes 1 Kugelhopf

350 g (12 oz) plain flour
generous pinch of salt
30 ml (2 tbsp) caster sugar
10 ml (2 tsp) instant dried yeast
100 g (3½ oz) butter or margarine
250 ml (8 fl oz) milk
2 eggs, beaten
few drops of vanilla essence
45 g (1½ oz) seedless raisins
45 g (1½ oz) currants
60 g (2 oz) flaked almonds, toasted
icing sugar

Combine flour, salt and sugar and microwave on 100% for 20 seconds. Turn into a mixing bowl and stir in yeast. Microwave butter for 45 seconds, or until melted but not boiling. Microwave milk for 45 seconds, or until lukewarm. Add milk to dry ingredients, beating well for 1 minute. Add butter, beaten eggs and vanilla and mix to a soft batter. Add raisins and currants and mix well. Grease a deep, microwave ring mould or pan and arrange toasted almonds in the base and sides of the mould. Carefully turn in the batter, spreading evenly. Cover loosely with plastic wrap and microwave for 15 seconds on 100%. Stand in the microwave for 8-10 minutes, then microwave again for 15 seconds. Repeat standing and microwaving until batter has doubled in volume. Remove plastic wrap and microwave for 7-9 minutes. Stand for 10 minutes before turning out onto a wire rack to cool. When cool, dust generously with icing sugar.

Seed Loaves

SEED LOAVES

Combination baking
Makes 4 small loaves

Bake the bread in four small soufflé dishes or in two clay flower-pots for an unusual effect.

15 ml (1 tbsp) instant dried yeast
750 g (1¾ lb) plain flour
30 ml (2 tbsp) sugar
10 ml (2 tsp) salt
500 ml (16 fl oz) warm milk
45 ml (3 tbsp) grated Parmesan cheese
60 ml (4 tbsp) soured cream
1 egg yolk
sesame seeds

Combine yeast, half the flour, the sugar and salt in a large mixing bowl. Add the warm milk and mix to combine, then beat for 3 minutes on medium speed. Add Parmesan cheese and soured cream, mixing well. Add enough of the remaining flour, a little at a time, to form a stiff dough. Knead until smooth and elastic, then cover and prove according to microwave directions. Knock down and divide dough into 4 portions. Shape each into a round and place in 4 small greased soufflé dishes. Cover and prove again. Brush tops with beaten egg yolk and sprinkle with sesame seeds. Place loaves in a circular pattern in the microwave. Bake as directed below or until loaves are golden brown and sound hollow when tapped. Remove bread from the dishes and cool on wire racks. Slice crossways to serve.

BROTHER
Hi-Speed at 190 °C for 16-20 minutes.

STOLLEN

100%...5 minutes
plus Combination baking
Serves 8

90 g (3 oz) sultanas
75 g (2½ oz) currants
90 g (3 oz) mixed peel
90 g (3 oz) glacé cherries, halved
75 ml (2½ fl oz) dark rum
400 g (14 oz) bread mix
30 g (1 oz) butter
150 ml (5 fl oz) water
100 ml (3½ fl oz) milk
1 egg, lightly beaten
45 g (1½ oz) flaked almonds
10 ml (2 tsp) melted butter
icing sugar

Place fruits in a bowl, add rum, microwave on 100% for 1 minute. Allow to stand for 1 hour. Drain, dry well with paper towel. Empty the bread mix into a large mixing bowl. Microwave butter for 45 seconds in a jug, then add the water and milk to the jug, microwave for 1-1½ minutes, until blood heat. Add egg to liquid, then using a dough hook mix the liquid into the bread mix to form a soft and pliable dough. Knead for about 4 minutes. Place dough in a lightly greased plastic bag, microwave for 15 seconds, rest dough for 7 minutes. Knead in the fruit and the nuts, roll mixture out into a rectangular shape, then roll up lengthways as for a Swiss roll. Place join securely underneath. Place seam-side down on a greased baking sheet, cover with plastic wrap, microwave for 15 seconds. Stand for 10 minutes, then repeat process twice more. Brush with melted butter and bake according to instructions below, or until golden brown and hollow-sounding when tapped. Remove from oven and cool on a wire rack. Sprinkle generously with sifted icing sugar.

BROTHER
Hi-Speed at 200 °C for 14-16 minutes.

BEESTING CAKE

100%, 50%...9 minutes
plus Convection baking
Serves 8-10

CAKE
60 ml (4 tbsp) water
30 ml (2 tbsp) milk
2.5 ml (½ tsp) dried yeast
30 ml (2 tbsp) sugar
225 g (8 oz) plain flour
generous pinch of salt
45 g (1½ oz) butter
pinch of grated lemon rind
TOPPING
45 g (1½ oz) chopped almonds
45 g (1½ oz) sugar
few drops of vanilla essence
15 ml (1 tbsp) honey
FILLING
30 g (1 oz) butter
45 g (1½ oz) plain flour
150 ml (5 fl oz) milk
2 egg yolks
30 g (1 oz) sugar
few drops of vanilla essence
100 ml (3½ fl oz) whipping cream
1 egg white

Combine water and milk in a small jug, microwave on 100% for about 45 seconds, until lukewarm. Add yeast and 5 ml (1 tsp) of the sugar, stir until combined. Sprinkle with 30 ml (2 tbsp) of the measured flour. Cover with plastic wrap, microwave for 10 seconds on 50%. Rest for 3 minutes, then repeat. A frothy fermentation will start to form. Sift remaining flour and salt into a bowl, add butter and rub in. Now add remaining sugar and lemon rind, mix to combine. Pour in the liquid. Using a large mixer, knead until smooth – about 4 minutes. Add a little extra liquid if necessary. Place the dough in a lightly greased roasting bag, tie the end loosely with string. Microwave on 100% for 15 seconds, rest for 10 minutes. Repeat this 2-3 times until the dough has doubled in size. Knock down and roll the dough into a circle about 15-mm (¾-in) thick. Place on a greased baking sheet, and shape into a perfect round. Cover with plastic wrap and allow to rise in a warm place for 15 minutes.

For the topping, place all ingredients in a small bowl, place in the microwave on 50% for 3-4 minutes, until slightly oily in appearance. Spread this mixture over the well-risen dough, then bake at 200 °C (400 °F) for 20 minutes. Remove from the oven, allow to cool, then split in half.

To make the filling, place butter in a large jug, microwave on 100% for 30 seconds, stir in the flour. Pour in milk all at once, beating with a wire whisk. Microwave for 1½-2 minutes stirring every 30 seconds. Beat in yolks, sugar and vanilla, the mixture will be very thick at this point. Cover with greaseproof paper and allow to cool to room temperature. Beat cream until thick, fold into the custard. Beat egg whites until soft peaks form, fold into the custard. Use this mixture to fill the cake.

BUTTERED APPLE ROUND

100%, 50%...12 minutes
Serves 8-10

350 g (12 oz) plain flour
2.5 ml (½ tsp) salt
30 g (1 oz) sugar
7.5 ml (1½ tsp) instant dried yeast
60 ml (4 tbsp) water
125 ml (4 fl oz) milk
60 g (2 oz) butter
1 egg
FILLING
45 g (1½ oz) butter
75 g (2½ oz) sugar
60 g (2 oz) soft brown sugar
6 Marie biscuits, crushed
10 ml (2 tsp) ground cinnamon
generous pinch of ground nutmeg
2.5 ml (½ tsp) finely grated lemon rind
2 Granny Smith apples
10 ml (2 tsp) lemon juice

First make the dough. Sift the flour and salt into a large bowl, add sugar and yeast. Combine water and milk in a jug, microwave on 100% for 30 seconds or until blood heat. Microwave butter for 1 minute, add to liquid and then mix in the egg. Add the liquids to the flour to form a soft dough. Continue to knead until a smooth pliable dough forms, about 4 minutes in a large mixer or 1 minute in a food processor. Turn the dough into a lightly greased roasting bag, microwave for 15 seconds, then rest for 10 minutes. Repeat this process at least twice more until the dough has doubled in size. Knock down dough, knead and cover.

To make the filling, microwave butter in a small bowl for 45 seconds, cool slightly. Combine sugars, biscuit crumbs, spices and rind in a small bowl. Peel, core and slice apples into about 12 wedges each. Sprinkle wedges with lemon juice.

To assemble, divide the dough into quarters, then divide each quarter into 6, form into rounds. Dip each ball into butter and then into the crumb mixture, coating evenly. Arrange in a well-greased 25-cm (10-in) ring pan, alternately with apple slices. Repeat with a second layer of dough and apple. Cover and microwave for 15 seconds, stand for 10 minutes. Repeat if necessary. Remove cover. Sprinkle dough with any remaining crumbs. Microwave on 50% for 6 minutes. Then microwave on 100% for 1½-2 minutes. Stand for 5 minutes before turning out and serving. Serve in slices with or without butter.

SURPRISE SAVARIN

100%...23 minutes
Serves 8

150 ml (5 fl oz) milk
12.5 ml (2½ tsp) dried yeast
30 g (1 oz) caster sugar
250 g (9 oz) plain flour
pinch of salt
100 g (3½ oz) butter or margarine
2 eggs, lightly beaten
90 g (3 oz) smooth apricot jam
SYRUP
300 ml (10 fl oz) water
200 g (7 oz) sugar
60 ml (4 tbsp) rum
FILLING
60 g (2 oz) caster sugar
45 ml (3 tbsp) water
60 g (2 oz) unblanched almonds
250 ml (8 fl oz) whipping cream
200 g (7 oz) glacé fruit, chopped
30 ml (2 tbsp) rum
100 g (3½ oz) plain chocolate, grated

Pour milk into a jug, microwave on 100% for about 15 seconds, until blood heat. Add yeast and 5 ml (1 tsp) sugar, stir to combine. Sprinkle milk with 30 ml (2 tbsp) of the measured flour, cover with plastic wrap. Microwave for 10 seconds, then stand for 5 minutes. Repeat microwaving and standing time once more.

Buttered Apple Round

Sift remaining flour and salt into the work bowl of a food processor, add remaining sugar. Microwave butter for 30 seconds to soften. The butter should not be melted. Add very soft butter to eggs, beat lightly, then add to yeast mixture. Add to flour and process very well until a smooth batter forms. Grease or spray a 23-cm (9-in) ring pan very well, turn batter into mould and cover with vented plastic wrap. To prove the mixture, microwave on 100% for 10 seconds, rest for 10 minutes. Repeat microwaving and resting twice more. The mixture should rise to the top of the mould. Remove plastic wrap and microwave for 4½-6 minutes until just dry on top. Stand for 10 minutes before turning out onto a wire rack.

For the syrup, combine water and sugar in a jug, microwave for 10 minutes, stirring after 5 minutes. Cool slightly and add rum.

Place plate under the savarin, spoon syrup over until completely absorbed. Transfer to a serving plate and chill well. Place jam in a small bowl, microwave for 1-2 minutes, until warm. Brush savarin with jam.

To make the filling, combine sugar and water in a jug, microwave for 2-3 minutes, stirring once during cooking time. The mixture should be a good caramel colour. Place almonds on an oiled baking sheet, pour caramel over and allow to cool. Grind to a fine powder in a food processor. Whip cream until peaking consistency. Now fold in remaining ingredients, including almond powder, pile cream mixture in the centre of the savarin. Chill well.

QUICK BREADS

Sweetcorn Bread, Cheese & Tomato Loaves, Individual Yorkshire Puddings

QUICK BREADS include scones, American muffins, griddle scones, tea breads, coffee cakes and other delicious bread mixtures that are made without yeast. These breads do not need time to prove, so are ideal for microwave baking. Many quick bread recipes include brown sugar, treacle, nuts and dried fruit, or wholemeal flour to give the finished breads a good colour. Some quick breads are savoury and include cheese, bacon and herbs while others are sweeter and incorporate fresh fruit and nuts. Traditionally, these quick breads are baked in rectangular loaf pans and although these are available for microwave baking, it is advisable to use a ring or round pan for more even baking.

CORNBREAD

100%, 70%...9 minutes
Makes 1 loaf

A quick bread with a difference to serve with a barbecue.

4 streaky bacon rashers, rinds removed and chopped
melted butter
60 g (2 oz) plain flour
12.5 ml (2½ tsp) baking powder
generous pinch of salt
15 ml (1 tbsp) sugar
350 g (12 oz) yellow polenta
30 ml (2 tbsp) chopped chives
2 eggs
150 ml (5 fl oz) milk

Place bacon in the base of a 20 cm (8-in) shallow casserole. Cover with waxed paper and microwave on 100% for 3 minutes. Drain bacon and reserve. Pour most of the bacon fat into a measuring jug and add sufficient butter to measure 60 ml (4 tbsp). Brush remaining bacon fat up around the sides of the casserole dish. Sift flour, baking powder and salt into a mixing bowl, add sugar, polenta, bacon and chives. Mix together eggs, milk and measured fat. Combine with the dry ingredients. Do not mix in well, the batter should still be slightly lumpy. Microwave prepared dish for 30 seconds, spoon in batter and cover with vented plastic wrap. Microwave for 5 minutes on 70%. Serve cut in wedges with butter.

SESAME YOGHURT BREAD

100%...8 minutes
Makes 1 loaf

60 g (2 oz) plain flour
60 g (2 oz) cornmeal
75 g (2½ oz) wholemeal flour
5 ml (1 tsp) bicarbonate of soda
2.5 ml (½ tsp) salt
1 egg
250 ml (8 fl oz) natural yoghurt
90 g (3 oz) molasses
20 ml (4 tsp) oil
45 ml (3 tbsp) natural sesame seeds

Combine dry ingredients in a large mixing bowl. Mix together egg, yoghurt, molasses and oil, add to dry ingredients, mixing well to moisten. Add about 30 ml (2 tbsp) of the sesame seeds to this mixture. Grease a small microwave ring pan, a flexible plastic container or small loaf pan and sprinkle with remaining sesame seeds. Spoon in the bread mixture and sprinkle with remaining seeds. Microwave on 100% for 5½-7½ minutes or until a skewer inserted in centre comes out clean. Stand for 10 minutes, then invert onto a wire rack to cool.

CHEESE & TOMATO LOAVES

Combination baking
Makes 4 small loaves

These mini loaves are easy to make and impressive to serve.

200 g (7 oz) plain flour
10 ml (2 tsp) baking powder
2.5 ml (½ tsp) bicarbonate of soda
185 ml (6 fl oz) tomato juice
1 egg
75 ml (2½ fl oz) oil
30 g (1 oz) caster sugar
2.5 ml (½ tsp) salt
45 ml (3 tbsp) chopped spring onion
100 g (3½ oz) Cheddar cheese, cubed

Sift the flour, baking powder and bicarbonate of soda into a mixing bowl and set aside. Combine the tomato juice, egg, oil, sugar, salt, spring onion and cheese in the container of an electric blender and blend until cheese is finely chopped. Pour tomato mixture over dry ingredients and mix until just moistened. Spoon mixture into 4 well-greased mini loaf pans and bake according to instructions below, until loaves are well risen and a wooden skewer inserted in the centre comes out clean. Turn out and cool on wire racks.

BROTHER
Hi-Speed at 180 °C for 15-19 minutes.

NOTE Consult the instruction book of your combination microwave for directions on using trivets and metal pans.

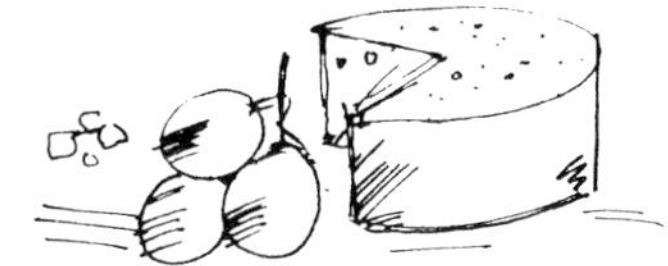

SWEETCORN BREAD

70%...10 minutes
Makes 1 loaf

45 ml (3 tbsp) toasted breadcrumbs (page 93)
150 g (5 oz) plain flour
10 ml (2 tsp) baking powder
5 ml (1 tsp) bicarbonate of soda
5 ml (1 tsp) salt
generous pinch of paprika
60 g (2 oz) margarine
3 eggs, lightly beaten
400 g (14 oz) canned whole kernel sweetcorn, drained
45 ml (3 tbsp) milk
30 g (1 oz) Cheddar cheese, grated

Grease a 25 × 12-cm (10 × 5-in) microwave loaf pan, coat the sides and base with crumbs. Sift the dry ingredients in a bowl and rub in the margarine. Combine eggs, sweetcorn and milk in a jug, pour into flour mixture and mix until just combined. Turn into the prepared pan, sprinkle with cheese and cover with plastic wrap. Microwave on 70% for 8-10 minutes. Uncover and stand for about 5 minutes before turning out.

SCONE-BASED PIZZA

100%...5 minutes
Serves 4-6

125 g (4 oz) plain flour
2.5 ml (½ tsp) cream of tartar
generous pinch of bicarbonate of soda
generous pinch of dried oregano
30 g (1 oz) margarine
60 ml (4 tbsp) milk
350 ml (11 fl oz) tomato topping (page 93)
100 g (3½ oz) Cheddar cheese, grated
a few black olives
30 g (1 oz) canned anchovies

To make the base, sift the dry ingredients. Add oregano and margarine, rub in. Mix to a moist scone dough consistency with the milk. Grease a 20-cm (8-in) pie plate or pizza plate and press the dough to fit. Microwave on 100% for 2 minutes. Spread topping over the dough. Sprinkle with cheese, dot with olives and pieces of anchovy. Microwave on 100% for 3 minutes. Stand for 2 minutes before serving.

SPICY COURGETTE BREAD

70%... 12 minutes
Makes 1 loaf

45 g (1½ oz) pecan nuts
2.5-cm (1-in) piece lemon peel
3 medium courgettes, trimmed
1 egg
125 ml (4 fl oz) oil
200 g (7 oz) plain flour
150 g (5 oz) sugar
5 ml (1 tsp) cinnamon
2.5 ml (½ tsp) ground nutmeg
pinch of ground cloves
2.5 ml (½ tsp) each salt, baking powder and bicarbonate of soda

Chop nuts and lemon peel in a food processor and set aside. Grate courgettes and set aside. Beat egg and oil until well mixed. Beat in courgettes and then add remaining ingredients, mixing until combined. Turn mixture into a well-greased 20-cm (8-in) ring pan and microwave on 70% for 10-12 minutes, or until a wooden skewer inserted near the centre comes out clean. Stand in the dish for about 5 minutes, then turn out on a wire rack to cool.

INDIVIDUAL YORKSHIRE PUDDINGS

Combination baking
Makes 6

15 ml (1 tbsp) oil
275 ml (9 fl oz) milk
2 eggs
pinch of salt
100 g (3½ oz) plain flour

Grease 6 custard cups or ramekins with oil. Place the remaining ingredients in a blender, blend until smooth, scraping down the edges of the goblet once. Divide batter between cups, arrange cups in a circle in the microwave. Microwave according to instructions below.

BROTHER
Preheat for 5 minutes on 250 °C. Bake on Hi-Speed at 250 °C for 3½ minutes, then on Turbo for 5 minutes.

Spicy Courgette Bread

APRICOT PECAN BREAD

70%...10 minutes
Makes 1 loaf

100 g (3½ oz) pecan nuts, finely chopped
150 g (5 oz) wholemeal flour
125 ml (4 fl oz) milk
60 g (2 oz) dried apricots, chopped
75 ml (2½ fl oz) oil
60 g (2 oz) sugar
60 ml (4 tbsp) honey
1 egg
10 ml (2 tsp) grated orange rind
2.5 ml (½ tsp) cinnamon
10 ml (2 tsp) baking powder
2.5 ml (½ tsp)salt

Grease a 1.5-litre (2¾-pint) glass ring dish and coat with half the nuts. Combine the remaining ingredients and mix well. Spoon the mixture into the prepared dish and microwave on 70% for 8-10 minutes or until a wooden cocktail stick inserted in the centre comes out clean. Allow to stand for about 8 minutes before turning out onto a wire rack to cool. Cool completely before slicing.

CARAMELIZED SCONE RING

100%...6 minutes
Makes 1 ring

5 ml (1 tsp) cinnamon
45 g (1½ oz) margarine
45 g (1½ oz) chopped pecan nuts
75 g (2½ oz) soft brown sugar
75 g (2½ oz) mixed dried fruit
30 ml (2 tbsp) honey
5 ml (1 tsp) grated orange rind
30 ml (2 tbsp) orange juice
225 g (8 oz) self-raising flour
generous pinch of baking powder
generous pinch of salt
5 ml (1 tsp) cinnamon
2.5 ml (½ tsp) ground nutmeg
generous pinch of ground cloves
30 g (1 oz) caster sugar
30 g (1 oz) margarine
1 egg, lightly beaten
100 ml (3½ fl oz) milk
30 g (1 oz) margarine, melted
extra cinnamon for dusting

Sprinkle a well-greased 20-23-cm (8-9-in) ring pan with cinnamon. Microwave margarine on 100% for 30 seconds. Add nuts, brown sugar, dried fruit, honey, orange rind and juice, mix to combine and set aside. Sift flour, baking powder, salt and spices, add caster sugar and rub in the margarine until the mixture resembles fine breadcrumbs. Mix the egg and milk, add to the mixture to form a soft pliable dough. Turn out onto a floured surface. Roll into a 23 × 15-cm (9 × 6-in) rectangle. Sprinkle dried fruit mixture over the dough, roll up Swiss roll fashion, starting at the long edge. Cut into 2.5-cm (1-in) thick slices, arrange in pan with the spiral pattern upwards. Brush with melted margarine and sprinkle with a little cinnamon. Microwave on 100% for 5 minutes. Stand for 5 minutes before turning out. Serve warm with or without butter.

FRUIT & BRAN LOAF

Combination baking
Makes 1 loaf

A rich quick bread, full of the goodness of dried fruit.

300 ml (10 fl oz) single cream
10 ml (2 tsp) lemon juice
2 eggs
60 g (2 oz) butter, melted
125 g (4 oz) mixed dried fruit, chopped
90 g (3 oz) All-Bran cereal
100 g (3½ oz) raisins or sultanas
200 g (7 oz) soft brown sugar
100 g (3½ oz) wholemeal flour
60 g (2 oz) plain flour
15 ml (1 tbsp) baking powder
2.5 ml (½ tsp) salt

Beat cream, lemon juice, eggs, melted butter and dried fruit together. Add All-Bran cereal, sultanas or raisins and brown sugar, mixing well. Combine flours, baking powder and salt and stir into the fruit mixture. Turn into a greased, square or rectangular loaf tin and bake according to directions below, until the loaf is well risen and a wooden skewer inserted in the centre comes out clean. Turn out and cool on a wire rack. Serve with plenty of butter.

BROTHER
Hi-Speed at 190 °C for 25-32 minutes.

BRAN RUSKS

100%, 70%, 15%...64 minutes
Makes about 20

125 g (4 oz) sunflower seeds
400 g (14 oz) plain flour
60 g (2 oz) All-Bran cereal
150 g (5 oz) soft brown sugar
20 ml (4 tsp) baking powder
2.5 ml (½ tsp) salt
250 g (9 oz) margarine
2 eggs
185 ml (6 fl oz) milk

Microwave a browning dish on 100% for 5 minutes, sprinkle sunflower seeds onto the dish and stir. Microwave for 1-2 minutes more, stirring every 30 seconds. Sift flour into a large bowl, add sunflower seeds, All-Bran, sugar, baking powder and salt. Cut margarine into small blocks, add to mixture and rub in. Lightly beat eggs and milk, add to mixture to form a soft workable dough. Grease or spray a rectangular 30 × 20-cm (12 × 8-in) dish, line the base with paper towel or plastic wrap.

Grease hands with a little margarine. Roll large, walnut-sized pieces of dough into finger shapes. Arrange in rows, leaving space between each ball to allow for rising. Microwave on 100% for 7 minutes, then reduce power to 70% and bake for a further 20-25 minutes. Stand for 5 minutes, then break into rusks. The rusks will still be slightly soft when they come out of the microwave, but will become crisp as they cool.

To dry rusks, place the baked rusks on a microwave baking sheet, cover with waxed paper. Microwave on 15% for 20-25 minutes, rearranging the rusks every 5 minutes. Cool and store.

OATCAKES

100%... 11 minutes
Makes about 18

These oatcakes should be light and crisp. Be careful not to overcook them.

15 g (½ oz) margarine
125 g (4 oz) porridge oats
2.5 ml (½ tsp) salt
2.5 ml (½ tsp) bicarbonate of soda
2.5 ml (½ tsp) dried mixed herbs (optional)
about 75 ml (2½ fl oz) hot water
extra porridge oats

Combine margarine, oats, salt, bicarbonate of soda and mixed herbs in a mixing bowl. Add enough of the water to make a stiff dough. Roll out very thinly on a surface sprinkled with extra oats. Cut into 6-cm (2½-in) rounds, re-rolling dough as needed. Place 6 rounds in a circular pattern in the microwave oven and microwave on 100% for 1½ minutes. Turn oatcakes over and microwave a further 1-2 minutes until dry. Place on a wire rack to cool and repeat with the remaining rounds. Store in an airtight container. Serve with cheese and cheese spreads.

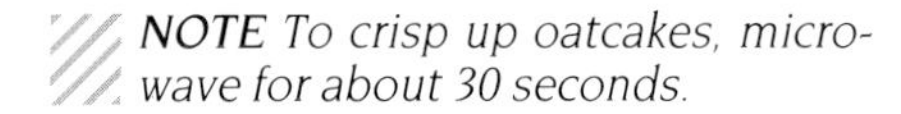

NOTE To crisp up oatcakes, microwave for about 30 seconds.

GRIDDLE SCONES

100%... 14 minutes
Makes 8 portions

Use a microwave browning dish to make these nicely browned griddle scones.

250 g (9 oz) plain flour
15 ml (1 tbsp) baking powder
7.5 ml (1½ tsp) salt
15 g (½ oz) butter
30 g (1 oz) sugar
150 ml (5 fl oz) milk

Heat a large browning dish on 100% for 4 minutes. Sift flour, baking powder and salt into a bowl. Rub in butter and mix in sugar. Add enough milk to make a soft dough. Turn out on a lightly floured board and knead gently. Divide dough in half and pat each half into a 5-mm

(¼-in) thick round. Cut each round into quarters. Be sure the browning dish is not too hot as it can scorch the scones. Place 4 quarters on the browning dish and microwave for 1½ minutes. Turn scones and microwave for 2-2½ minutes longer. To bake remaining scones, wipe browning dish clean with paper towel and reheat for 1-2 minutes, then repeat the baking. Serve warm.

VARIATIONS

☐ Substitute buttermilk for milk.
☐ Omit sugar and add 5 ml (1 tsp) dried herbs of your own choice, and 30 ml (1 tbsp) finely grated cheese.

SCONES

100%... 6 minutes
Makes 12

90 g (3 oz) butter or margarine
250 g (9 oz) plain flour
15 ml (1 tbsp) baking powder
2.5 ml (½ tsp) salt
30 g (1 oz) sugar (for sweet scones only)
1 egg
about 185 ml (6½ fl oz) milk

TOPPING FOR SWEET SCONES
a little melted butter
30 g (1 oz) sugar
5 ml (1 tsp) cinnamon

TOPPING FOR SAVOURY SCONES
15 ml (1 tbsp) melted butter
generous pinch of paprika

Rub butter into the flour, baking powder and salt until mixture resembles fine crumbs. Stir in sugar if making sweet scones. Combine egg and milk, and add enough liquid to the dry ingredients to form a stiff dough. Roll or pat dough to about 1-cm (½-in) thickness. Cut into rounds and arrange 6 scones at a time on a plate lined with double thickness of paper towel.

For sweet scones, brush with melted butter and sprinkle with a combination of the sugar and cinnamon. For savoury scones, combine melted butter and paprika and brush over the tops of the scones.

Microwave on 100% for 2-3 minutes, or until no longer doughy. Stand 1 minute, then remove to a wire rack. Repeat with remaining scones.

If desired, omit toppings and brush tops of microwaved scones with a little melted butter. Place under a hot grill to brown the tops.

VARIATIONS

Fruit scones Add 45 g (1½ oz) raisins or sultanas to the dry ingredients before adding the liquid. Proceed as above.

Wheat germ scones Substitute 60 ml (4 tbsp) wheat germ for 60 ml (4 tbsp) of the flour and proceed as above.

Savoury scones Add 60 g (2 oz) grated Cheddar cheese and 5 ml (1 tsp) mixed dried herbs to the dry ingredients before adding the liquid. Proceed as above.

Wholemeal scones Substitute 125 g (4 oz) wholemeal flour for 125 g (4 oz) plain flour in the recipe and proceed as above.

NOTE To microwave Scones in a browning dish, prepare scone mixture as above. Preheat a browning dish for 4 minutes on 100%. Grease with a little oil and heat 30 seconds more. Place 6 scones in a circle on the dish and microwave on 100% for 2-3 minutes.

DATE LOAF

100%... 12 minutes
Makes 1 loaf

60 g (2 oz) margarine
250 g (9 oz) dates, cut up
200 g (7 oz) soft brown sugar
250 ml (8 fl oz) water
5 ml (1 tsp) bicarbonate of soda
1 egg
250 g (9 oz) plain flour

Place the margarine, dates, sugar and water in a large bowl. Microwave on 100% for 4 minutes, stirring once during the cooking time. Stir in bicarbonate of soda and allow to cool. Lightly beat egg and add to the mixture. Mix in sifted flour. Line a 25 × 12-cm (10 × 5-in) loaf pan with paper towel or grease pan well. Pour loaf mixture in and microwave on 100% for 6-8 minutes. Allow to cool in the pan. Serve plain or with butter.

Centre *Cheesy American Muffins;* left *Date & Orange American Muffins*

DATE & ORANGE AMERICAN MUFFINS

100%, 50%...22 minutes
Makes about 24

30 g (1 oz) margarine
200 g (7 oz) soft brown sugar
1 egg
125 ml (4 fl oz) water
125 ml (4 fl oz) orange juice
2.5 ml (½ tsp) finely grated orange rind
125 g (4 oz) dates, chopped
250 g (9 oz) wholemeal flour
5 ml (1 tsp) bicarbonate of soda
5 ml (1 tsp) baking powder

Beat margarine, brown sugar and egg together. Place water, orange juice, rind and dates in a bowl, microwave on 100% for 2 minutes, cool slightly.

Add wholemeal flour, bicarbonate of soda and baking powder, then stir in the sugar mixture.

Line a microwave patty pan with paper cases, spoon in about 25 ml (5 tsp) of the mixture per muffin. Microwave 6 muffins at a time on 50% for 4-5 minutes. Cool slightly, then split and serve with butter.

CHEESY AMERICAN MUFFINS

Combination baking
Makes 12 large muffins

90 g (3 oz) All-Bran cereal
300 ml (10 fl oz) milk
100 ml (3½ fl oz) oil
2 eggs
2.5 ml (½ tsp) dried oregano
2.5 ml (½ tsp) dried thyme
2.5 ml (½ tsp) paprika
2.5 ml (½ tsp) salt
250 g (9 oz) plain flour
15 ml (1 tbsp) chopped chives
15 ml (1 tbsp) chopped fresh parsley
30 ml (2 tbsp) grated Parmesan cheese
45 g (1½ oz) Cheddar cheese, grated
paprika

Soak cereal in milk for about 10 minutes. Beat oil, eggs and herbs together lightly with a fork. Sift the dry ingredients together. Add bran mixture to the oil mixture, beat well, then stir in the flour, chives, parsley and Parmesan cheese. Spoon about 45 ml (3 tbsp) of the mixture into well-greased muffin pans. Sprinkle with Cheddar cheese and dust with paprika. Bake according to the chart below.

BROTHER
Preheat for 7 minutes on 250 °C.
Bake on Hi-Speed for 3½ minutes, then Turbo for 5 minutes.

SWEET TARTS

Pumpkin Rum Pie

IT HAS been said that the true test of a good cook is the making of fine pastry. Shortcrust and suet pastries become tender and flaky when baked by microwave energy but do not brown. Brushing the uncooked pastry shell with a little egg yolk or vanilla essence mixed with water, or adding a few drops of yellow food colouring to the dough, will improve the colour. Crumb crusts can be baked quickly and easily in a microwave oven, in fact the butter or margarine can be melted directly in the pie plate. Pastries such as choux or puff need hot dry air to give their characteristic finish and are not suitable for baking by microwave energy alone but do very well when baked in a combination oven.

PUMPKIN PIE

100%, 50%... 15 minutes
Makes 1 × 23-cm (9-in) pie

1 × 23-cm (9-in) shortcrust pastry shell, baked (page 87)
450 g (1 lb) cooked, mashed pumpkin
400 g (14 oz) canned condensed milk
60 g (2 oz) soft brown sugar
60 ml (4 tbsp) water
1 egg
15 ml (1 tbsp) plain flour
2.5 ml (½ tsp) ground ginger
5 ml (1 tsp) cinnamon
2.5 ml (½ tsp) ground allspice
pinch of ground cloves
pinch of salt
whipped cream to serve

Combine pumpkin, condensed milk, sugar, water, egg, flour, spices and salt in a large bowl. Beat until smooth. Microwave on 100% for 6 minutes, stirring every minute. Pour mixture into pastry shell, microwave on 50% for 9 minutes. Allow to stand until cool before serving with whipped cream.

PINEAPPLE MERINGUE PIE

100%, 70%... 10 minutes
plus Grill
Makes 1 × 23-cm (9-in) pie

1 × 23-cm (9-in) shortcrust pastry shell, baked (page 87) or crumb crust (page 86)

FILLING
400 g (14 oz) canned crushed pineapple
1 egg yolk
30 ml (2 tbsp) custard powder
15 ml (1 tbsp) cornflour
60 ml (4 tbsp) orange juice
2.5 ml (½ tsp) grated orange rind
15 ml (1 tbsp) orange liqueur
60 g (2 oz) butter

MERINGUE
3 egg whites
60 g (2 oz) caster sugar
60 g (2 oz) icing sugar

Place undrained pineapple in a bowl, microwave on 100% for 3 minutes. Beat egg yolk, custard powder and cornflour until smooth, add orange juice, beat again. Add a little of the hot pineapple to this, then return all the mixture to the pineapple. Microwave for 2 minutes, stirring every 30 seconds. Stir in rind, orange liqueur and butter. Cool completely, then spoon into prepared shell. Beat egg whites until stiff peaks form. Combine sugars, and beat into egg whites 5 ml (1 tsp) at a time. Spread in peaks on top of filling. Microwave on 70% for 5 minutes. To brown, place under a hot grill for 2-3 minutes. Serve at room temperature.

COCONUT MERINGUE PIE

100%, 70%... 13 minutes
plus Convection baking
Makes 1 × 23-cm (9-in) pie

CRUST
75 g (2½ oz) desiccated coconut, toasted
100 g (3½ oz) Marie biscuit crumbs
30 g (1 oz) soft brown sugar
2.5 ml (½ tsp) cinnamon
75 g (2½ oz) butter or margarine
45 ml (3 tbsp) single cream

FILLING
100 g (3½ oz) sugar
15 g (½ oz) plain flour
15 g (½ oz) cornflour
500 ml (16 fl oz) milk
4 egg yolks
45 g (1½ oz) desiccated coconut
15 g (½ oz) butter or margarine
few drops of vanilla essence
few drops of caramel essence

MERINGUE
4 egg whites
5 ml (1 tsp) cornflour
generous pinch of cream of tartar
75 g (2½ oz) sugar
few drops of vanilla essence
toasted coconut

To make the crust, combine coconut, biscuit crumbs, sugar and cinnamon. Microwave butter for 45 seconds on 100% and add to crumb mixture along with the cream. Mix well and press into bottom and sides of a 23-cm (9-in) pie plate. Microwave on 70% for 2 minutes, then allow to cool.

For the filling, mix together the sugar, flour, cornflour and milk. Microwave on 100% for 6-8 minutes, stirring every minute until thickened. Beat egg yolks, then stir in half the hot mixture. Return to the remaining hot mixture and beat well. Stir in coconut. Microwave for 1-2 minutes to heat through and thicken. Stir in butter, vanilla and caramel essence. Pour into prepared crust.

For the meringue, beat egg whites, cornflour and cream of tartar until frothy. Gradually add the sugar, beating until very stiff. Mix in vanilla. Pile meringue on top of the pie and sprinkle with toasted coconut. Place in a preheated convection oven at 180 °C (350 °F) for 10-12 minutes, or until golden brown. Cool before serving.

PUMPKIN RUM PIE

Combination baking
Makes 1 × 23-cm (9-in) pie

1 × 23-cm (9-in) shortcrust pastry shell, uncooked (page 87)
350 g(12 oz) cooked, mashed pumpkin
100 g (3½ oz) sugar
45 g (1½ oz) soft brown sugar
generous pinch of salt
5 ml (1 tsp) cinnamon
2.5 ml (½ tsp) ground ginger
2.5 ml (½ tsp) ground nutmeg
generous pinch of ground cloves
3 eggs, lightly beaten
300 ml (10 fl oz) milk
185 ml (6 fl oz) evaporated milk
30 ml (2 tbsp) dark rum
45 g (1½ oz) pecan nuts, coarsely chopped (optional)

Combine pumpkin, sugars, salt and spices, mixing well. Stir in eggs, milk and evaporated milk. Add rum and mix well. Pour into prepared pastry shell and sprinkle with pecans if using. Bake according to instructions below. Cool, then cut into wedges to serve.

BROTHER
Hi-Speed at 200 °C for 20-24 minutes.

Lemon & Coconut Tart

LEMON & COCONUT TART

70%...4 minutes
plus Combination and
Convection baking
Makes 1 × 20-cm (8-in) tart

200 g (7 oz) vanilla cake mix
1 egg
200 ml (6½ fl oz) water
500 ml (16 fl oz) milk
3 eggs, separated
250 g (9 oz) caster sugar
15 ml (1 tbsp) grated lemon rind
90 ml (3 fl oz) lemon juice
60 g (2 oz) desiccated coconut

Beat the cake mix with egg and water until well mixed. Turn into a well-greased and lined 20-cm (8-in) pie plate and microwave on 70% for 3-4 minutes, or until just firm. Stand until cool. Combine the milk, egg yolks, 150 g (5 oz) caster sugar, lemon rind and juice and the coconut, mixing well. When cake has cooled, crumble it into a mixing bowl and beat in the milk mixture. Turn into a deep, 20-cm (8-in) ovenproof dish and bake according to instructions below. Beat egg whites to soft peaks, then gradually beat in the remaining caster sugar. Pile the meringue on top of the lemon mixture and bake on convection at 180 °C (350 °F) for about 10 minutes or until lightly browned. Serve warm or cold.

BROTHER
Hi-Speed at 180 °C for 20-25 minutes, or until just set.

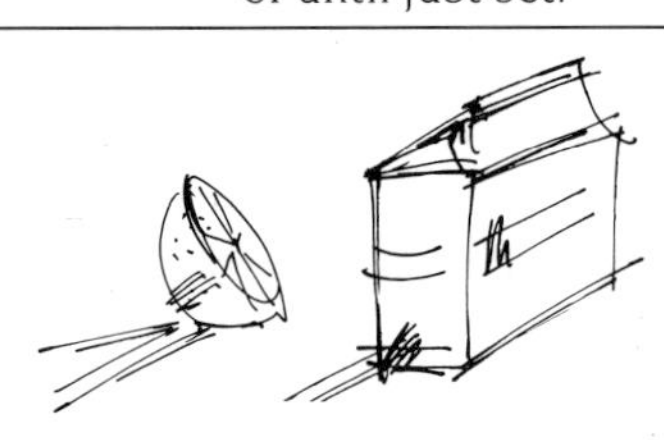

PECAN CHOCOLATE PIE

50%...2 minutes
plus Combination baking
Makes 1 × 23-cm (9-in) pie

75 g (2½ oz) pecan nuts
60 g (2 oz) plain chocolate
3 eggs
30 ml (2 tbsp) milk
few drops of vanilla essence
100 g (3½ oz) soft brown sugar
100 g (3½ oz) sugar
15 g (½ oz) plain flour
125 g (4 oz) butter or margarine, softened
30 ml (2 tbsp) desiccated coconut, toasted

Place two-thirds of the nuts in a blender and blend until finely ground. Press into the bottom and sides of a well-greased 23-cm (9-in) pie plate. Chop the remaining nuts and set aside.

Microwave chocolate on 50% for 2 minutes or until melted, stirring frequently. Place eggs, milk, vanilla, sugars, flour and butter in the blender and blend until smooth. Add melted chocolate and blend until well mixed. Mix in coconut and carefully pour into prepared dish. Sprinkle with remaining nuts. Bake according to instructions below, then cool and chill.

BROTHER
Hi-Speed at 160 °C for 14-16 minutes.

PECAN PIE

100%, 50%...20 minutes
Makes 1 × 23-cm (9-in) pie

1 × 23-cm (9-in) shortcrust pastry shell, uncooked (page 87)
1 egg yolk
30 ml (2 tbsp) golden syrup
60 g (2 oz) butter
3 eggs
1 extra egg white
350 g (12 oz) golden syrup
75 g (2½ oz) soft brown sugar
15 ml (1 tbsp) plain flour
few drops of vanilla essence
15 ml (1 tbsp) sherry
150 g (5 oz) pecan nuts

Brush the inside of the pastry shell with a mixture of egg yolk and syrup. Microwave on 100% for 4 minutes.

Microwave butter in a large bowl for 45 seconds. Add eggs and egg white and whisk well. Mix in syrup, sugar, flour, vanilla and sherry. Stir in the pecans. Pour into the pastry shell, microwave on 50% for 12-15 minutes. The top should be almost dry to the touch and well puffed. Cool, then cut into wedges.

PUMPKIN TARTLETS WITH GLAZED PECANS

100%, 70%...9 minutes
Makes 12

1 × recipe shortcrust pastry (page 87)
FILLING
1 egg
1 egg yolk
10 ml (2 tsp) plain flour
225 g (8 oz) cooked, mashed pumpkin
2.5 ml (½ tsp) mixed spice
75 ml (2½ fl oz) maple syrup
75 ml (2½ fl oz) single cream
60 ml (4 tbsp) milk
6 gingernut biscuits, crushed
GLAZE
60 ml (4 tbsp) maple syrup
10 ml (2 tsp) golden syrup
12 pecans
whipped cream to serve

Roll the pastry out thinly, then using a fluted cutter, cut 12 rounds to fit a microwave muffin pan. Spray or grease the muffin cups and carefully line with the pastry. Cut circles of waxed paper to fit the pastry shapes, add a few beans to prevent the pastry from rising. Microwave on 100% for 2-3 minutes.

To make the filling, beat egg, egg yolk and flour together, then beat in the pumpkin, mixed spice and syrup. Stir in cream and milk. Carefully spoon into lined cups. Microwave on 70% for 3½-4 minutes, until just set. Cool slightly before unmoulding. Sprinkle with crushed gingernut biscuits. Repeat with remaining pastry and filling. Serve decorated with glazed pecans and cream.

To glaze pecans, combine the syrups in a jug, microwave on 100% for 2 minutes. Carefully place pecan on a cocktail stick and dip into syrup. Place on an oiled baking sheet and allow to dry. Work quickly as the syrup sets quickly.

Pumpkin Tartlets With Glazed Pecans

SHERRY CREAM TART

100%...15 minutes
Makes 2 × 23-cm (9-in) tarts

1 packet chocolate cake mix
1 packet butterscotch instant pudding
125 ml (4 fl oz) water
125 ml (4 fl oz) oil
125 ml (4 fl oz) sweet sherry
4 eggs
pinch of ground nutmeg
2.5 ml (½ tsp) ground ginger
30 g (1 oz) desiccated coconut

SYRUP
100 g (3½ oz) margarine
45 ml (3 tbsp) water
125 g (4 oz) soft brown sugar
100 ml (3½ fl oz) sweet sherry
250 ml (8 fl oz) whipped cream to serve

Combine cake mix and instant pudding in a bowl. Beat water, oil, sherry and eggs lightly in a jug, add to dry ingredients and beat until well mixed, about 1 minute. Mix in spices. Pour mixture into 2 × 23-cm (9-in) pie plates, sprinkle with coconut. Microwave one at a time on 100% for 5-6 minutes. Cool slightly.

To make the syrup: Place all the ingredients, except cream, in a jug, microwave on 100% for 3 minutes, stirring at least once during the cooking time. Pour syrup over the top of the tarts. Serve warm or cold with whipped cream.

Sherry Cream Tart

MOCHA CREAM PIE

100%, 30%...4 minutes
Makes 1 × 23-cm (9-in) pie

1 × 23-cm (9-in) chocolate crumb crust (page 87)

FILLING
150 ml (5 fl oz) milk
25 marshmallows, halved
30 ml (2 tbsp) instant coffee granules
2 egg yolks
30 ml (2 tbsp) coffee liqueur
300 ml (10 fl oz) whipping cream
60 ml (4 tbsp) whipping cream, whipped, and grated chocolate to decorate

Microwave milk in a large jug on 100% for 2 minutes. Stir in marshmallows and coffee. Microwave on 30% for 2 minutes, stir to dissolve. Beat yolks well and beat into marshmallow mixture, add liqueur. Allow to cool to room temperature. Beat cream until thickening, fold into marshmallow mixture. Pour into prepared pie crust, chill until firm. Decorate with cream and grated chocolate.

APPLE & RAISIN CREAM PIE

Combination baking
Makes 1 × 23-cm (9-in) pie

2 × recipe shortcrust pastry (page 87)
egg white

FILLING
1.5 kg (3 lb) firm cooking apples
75 g (2½ oz) seedless raisins
30 ml (2 tbsp) fresh lemon juice
100 g (3½ oz) sugar
10 ml (2 tsp) cinnamon
2.5 ml (½ tsp) ground nutmeg
pinch of ground cloves
185 ml (6 fl oz) single cream
30 ml (2 tbsp) medium sherry

Divide pastry and roll half to fit a deep, 23-cm (9-in) pie plate. Roll remaining pastry and cut into thin strips to make the lattice top.

For the filling, peel and slice the apples, place in a large bowl with the raisins and sprinkle lemon juice over. Combine sugar, cinnamon, nutmeg and cloves and sprinkle over apples, tossing to coat. Mix cream and sherry and add to the apples. Brush the pastry shell with a little egg white and add the filling. Carefully fit the thin strips of pastry to make a lattice top. Seal edges well. Bake according to instructions below. Cool on a wire rack and serve warm or cold with cream or ice cream.

BROTHER
Hi-Speed at 200 °C for 20-26 minutes or until golden brown.

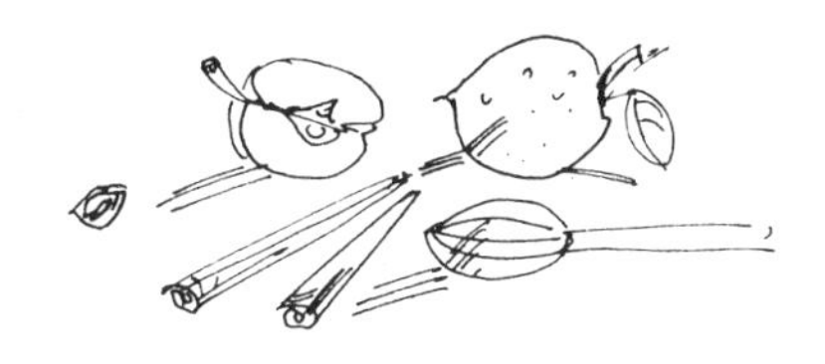

Apple & Raisin Cream Pie

DATE & BRANDY TART

70%... 18 minutes
Makes 1 × 23-cm (9-in) tart

225 g (8 oz) dates, chopped
60 g (2 oz) sultanas
2.5 ml (½ tsp) bicarbonate of soda
250 ml (8 fl oz) boiling water
2 eggs
200 g (7 oz) sugar
60 g (2 oz) margarine
200 g (7 oz) plain flour
60 g (2 oz) pecan nuts, chopped
SAUCE
175 g (6 oz) soft brown sugar
15 g (½ oz) margarine
250 ml (8 fl oz) boiling water
few drops of vanilla essence
125 ml (4 fl oz) brandy

Place dates, sultanas, bicarbonate of soda and boiling water in a bowl, set aside to cool. Beat eggs well, add half the sugar and beat well. Cream margarine and remaining sugar, combine both mixtures. Add date mixture and mix well. Sift flour, add to mixture about a third at a time, mixing well after each addition. Stir in the nuts. Pour into a greased 23-cm (9-in) pie plate. Microwave on 70% for 13-15 minutes. Allow to stand for 10 minutes.

To make the sauce, place all ingredients in a jug, microwave on 70% for 2-3 minutes, stirring at least once to dissolve the sugar. Carefully pour over the hot tart. Serve warm or cold with cream.

APRICOT & SULTANA TART

100%... 1 minute
plus Combination baking
Makes 1 × 20-cm (8-in) tart

125 g (4 oz) butter or margarine
few drops of vanilla essence
150 g (5 oz) desiccated coconut
60 g (2 oz) plain flour
60 g (2 oz) sugar
FILLING
400 g (14 oz) canned apricot halves, drained and coarsely chopped
60 g (2 oz) sultanas
pinch of nutmeg and ground cinnamon
45 ml (3 tbsp) single cream

Microwave butter on 100% for 1 minute. Stir in vanilla, coconut, flour and sugar. Press half the mixture into a 20-cm (8-in) pie plate.

Combine apricots, sultanas, cinnamon, nutmeg and cream, mixing well. Spread over the base and crumble the remaining butter mixture over the top. Bake according to instructions below. Serve warm with cream or ice cream.

BROTHER
Hi-Speed at 200 °C for 20-25 minutes or until nicely browned.

Brownie Pie With Ice Cream

BROWNIE PIE WITH ICE CREAM

100%... 6 minutes
Makes 1 × 23-cm (9-in) pie

90 g (3 oz) butter or margarine
75 g (2½ oz) sugar
75 ml (2½ fl oz) honey
few drops of vanilla essence
2 eggs
30 g (1 oz) wholemeal flour
45 g (1½ oz) wheat germ
45 g (1½ oz) cocoa powder
pinch of salt
strawberry or vanilla ice cream

Cream butter and sugar until light. Add honey and vanilla and beat well. Add eggs, one at a time, beating after each addition. Add flour, wheat germ, cocoa powder and salt and mix until just blended. Turn mixture into a greased, 23-cm (9-in) pie plate and microwave on 100% for 5-6 minutes, or until a skewer inserted near the centre comes out clean. The top should still be slightly moist. Cool, then cut into wedges and serve topped with ice cream.

Wholemeal Cherry Pie

WHOLEMEAL CHERRY PIE

Combination baking
Makes 1 × 23-cm (9-in) pie

1 × 23-cm (9-in) wholemeal pastry shell, uncooked (page 86)

FILLING
400 g (14 oz) canned cherry pie filling
2.5 ml (½ tsp) grated orange rind
15 ml (1 tbsp) Kirsch
1 Granny Smith apple, peeled and chopped

TOPPING
75 g (2½ oz) margarine
45 g (1½ oz) wholemeal flour
45 g (1½ oz) soft brown sugar
30 g (1 oz) bran

Line the pastry with greaseproof paper and fill with dried beans. Bake the pastry shell blind according to the instructions below. Remove paper and beans.

Combine all the ingredients for the filling, pour into the pastry shell.

Now make the topping. Rub the margarine into the flour, add remaining ingredients. Sprinkle over the top, bake according to instructions below. Cool slightly before serving with cream or custard. This pie is also delicious served chilled.

BROTHER
Hi-Speed at 200 °C for 5 minutes for the pastry shell and 12 minutes for the filling.

CRUSTLESS MILK TART

70%... 24 minutes
Makes 2 × 23-cm (9-in) tarts

200 g (7 oz) sugar
15 g (½ oz) butter, melted
4 eggs, separated
125 g (4 oz) plain flour
5 ml (1 tsp) baking powder
1 litre (1¾ pints) milk
few drops of vanilla essence
cinnamon

Beat sugar and butter together. Add yolks and mix again. Sift the dry ingredients and add alternately with the milk to the egg mixture. Stir in vanilla essence. Beat whites until peaking consistency, fold into mixture. Pour into two greased 23-cm (9-in) pie plates. Microwave each one on 70% for 10-12 minutes. Allow to stand for 15 minutes. Dust generously with cinnamon before serving.

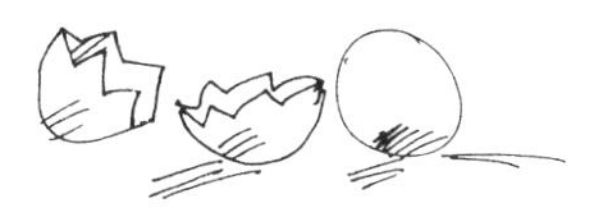

BISCUITS & BARS

Front *Peanut Raisin Bars;* left *Triple Chocolate Bars;* right *Apple Sauce Squares*

IN THIS chapter there is a wide selection of very special recipes for biscuits, bars and fancy cup cakes. Many of these recipes contain fruit, nuts, chocolate and other ingredients that give extra flavour. As it is very easy to overcook small cakes in the microwave oven, please take care with recipes in this section. Remember too that only a few biscuits can be baked at a time, so large batches will take longer to microwave than to bake conventionally. The texture and colour of microwaved biscuits differ somewhat from those baked in a conventional oven. Those baked in a combination microwave oven, however, will look similar to those baked conventionally, but because of the size of the oven, the number of biscuits baked at any one time is still limited.

CHOCOLATE & COCONUT BISCUITS

100%...8 minutes
Makes about 24 double biscuits

250 g (9 oz) margarine
200 g (7 oz) caster sugar
250 g (9 oz) self-raising flour
30 g (1 oz) cocoa powder
pinch of salt
150 g (5 oz) desiccated coconut
125 ml (4 fl oz) boiling water
5 ml (1 tsp) instant coffee granules
100 g (3½ oz) plain chocolate, chopped
1 × recipe chocolate icing (page 90)

Cream margarine and sugar until light and fluffy. Sift the dry ingredients into a bowl and add coconut. Combine water and instant coffee. Add one-third of the dry ingredients to the creamed mixture and beat to combine. Now add one-third of the coffee mixture and mix. Repeat until all the ingredients have been combined. Grease or line a microwave baking sheet with parchment paper. Roll dough into walnut-sized balls. Arrange on a baking sheet in a circle, leaving 5-mm (¼-in) between each ball. Microwave on 100% for 4-5 minutes. Lift off paper with a spatula and cool on a wire rack. Repeat until all the dough has been used, about 5 more batches.

When biscuits are cool, microwave chocolate on 100% for 2½-3 minutes, stirring at least once during the cooking time. Spread chocolate on the flat side of half the biscuits and spread icing on the rounded side of the other half. Sandwich one of each together.

PEANUT RAISIN BARS

100%...6 minutes
Makes 12-20

These bars are sticky and chewy and full of goodness.

30 g (1 oz) butter or margarine
200 g (7 oz) soft brown sugar
100 g (3½ oz) peanuts, coarsely chopped
75 g (2½ oz) seedless raisins
75 g (2½ oz) plain flour
45 ml (3 tbsp) porridge oats
pinch of bicarbonate of soda
pinch of salt
2 large eggs
few drops of vanilla essence
icing sugar

Microwave butter in a 20-cm (8-in) square baking dish. Combine brown sugar, nuts, raisins, flour, oats, bicarbonate of soda and salt. Mix well, then beat in eggs and vanilla. Spoon mixture over melted butter in the baking dish. Spread to edges but do not stir. Microwave on 100% for 5½-6 minutes. The mixture should still be moist in the centre. Allow to stand for 5 minutes, then sprinkle with icing sugar. Place a wire rack on a tray and turn out the bars. Cool, then sprinkle with icing sugar and cut into bars. Store in a single layer in an airtight container.

APPLE SAUCE SQUARES

70%...13 minutes
Makes 16

125 g (4 oz) margarine
200 g (7 oz) soft brown sugar
2 eggs
300 ml (10 fl oz) unsweetened apple sauce
90 g (3 oz) sultanas
175 g (6 oz) plain flour
2.5 ml (½ tsp) bicarbonate of soda
5 ml (1 tsp) cinnamon
generous pinch of ground cloves
generous pinch of ground allspice
generous pinch of salt
30 g (1 oz) icing sugar
2.5 ml (½ tsp) cinnamon

Line a 23-cm (9-in) square or rectangular dish with parchment paper or paper towel. Cream margarine and sugar together until light and fluffy. Add eggs one at a time and beat well. Combine apple sauce and sultanas, and add to creamed mixture. Sift dry ingredients, except icing sugar and cinnamon and add about one-third at a time to the creamed mixture. Pour into the prepared dish. Microwave on 70% for 11-13 minutes, until the top is just cooked. When cool, sprinkle with icing sugar and cinnamon. Cut into squares and serve plain or with cream.

TRIPLE LAYER CHOCOLATE SQUARES

100%...9 minutes
Makes 16

BASE
45 g (1½ oz) caster sugar
30 g (1 oz) cocoa powder
100 g (3½ oz) plain flour
generous pinch of baking powder
45 g (1½ oz) soft butter or margarine
few drops of vanilla essence
1 extra large egg

FILLING
300 ml (10 fl oz) evaporated milk
30 g (1 oz) cocoa powder
45 g (1½ oz) porridge oats
45 g(1½ oz) desiccated coconut
60 g (2 oz) icing sugar
30 g (1 oz) walnuts, chopped

TOPPING
150 g (5 oz) icing sugar
15 ml (1 tbsp) cocoa powder
15 g (½ oz) butter
30 ml (2 tbsp) boiling water

For the base, combine sugar, cocoa, flour, baking powder, butter, vanilla essence and egg. Beat well and spread in a greased 20-cm (8-in) baking dish. Microwave on 100% for 2-2½ minutes. Remove from oven.

For the filling, combine all ingredients except nuts and microwave for 5-6 minutes, stirring every minute. The mixture should be very thick. Stir in nuts. Spread evenly over the base and allow to cool.

For the topping, sift icing sugar. Combine cocoa and butter with boiling water and beat into the icing sugar. Spread over the filling and chill. Cut into squares to serve.

Top *Chocolate Pecan Brownies*; centre *Chocolate Chip Squares*; bottom *Marie Bars*

MARIE BARS

100%...7 minutes
Makes 20-24

200 g (7 oz) Marie biscuit crumbs
75 g (2½ oz) soft brown sugar
75 g (2½ oz) sugar
45 g (1½ oz) butter, melted
60 g (2 oz) plain chocolate
30 g (1 oz) hazelnuts, chopped
170 ml (5½ fl oz) evaporated milk
few drops of vanilla essence
15 g (½ oz) desiccated coconut

Combine crumbs and sugars, mix in butter. Break chocolate into small pieces and process in a food processor with the nuts until finely chopped. Add to the crumb mixture. Stir in milk, vanilla and coconut. Spread mixture in a greased 20-cm (8-in) baking dish. Microwave on 100% for 5-7 minutes. The top should appear dry. Allow to stand in the dish for 2 minutes, then loosen sides and turn out onto a wire rack to cool. Cut into bars to serve.

CHOCOLATE PECAN BROWNIES

70%, 50%...12 minutes
Makes 16-20

75 g (2½ oz) butter
150 g (5 oz) plain chocolate
200 g (7 oz) sugar
100 g (3½ oz) plain flour
2.5 ml (½ tsp) baking powder
2.5 ml (½ tsp) salt
2 eggs
45 g (1½ oz) pecan nuts, finely chopped

Place butter and 60 g (2 oz) plain chocolate in a 20-cm (8-in) baking dish. Microwave on 70% for 1-2 minutes until melted. Mix well then stir in the sugar, flour, baking powder, salt, eggs and nuts. Mix well. Grate remaining chocolate and fold into the batter. Spread batter evenly in dish. Shield corners of the dish with aluminium foil and microwave on 50% for 8-10 minutes, or until a skewer inserted about 2.5-cm (1-in) from the edge comes out clean. Cool on a heat-resistant surface and when cold cut into bars.

CHOCOLATE CHIP SQUARES

100%...6½ minutes
Makes 16-24

125 g (4 oz) butter, softened
150 g (5 oz) soft brown sugar
1 egg
15 ml (1 tbsp) milk
few drops of vanilla essence
150 g (5 oz) plain flour
2.5 ml (½ tsp) baking powder
generous pinch of cinnamon
pinch of salt
100 g (3½ oz) chocolate chips
45 g (1½ oz) nuts, chopped (optional)

Cream butter and sugar until light and fluffy. Add egg and beat well. Stir in milk and vanilla. Combine flour, baking powder, cinnamon and salt and add to the butter mixture. Mix well, then stir in chocolate chips and nuts. Turn the mixture into a greased 20-cm (8-in) baking dish and shield corners of dish with small pieces of foil. Microwave on 100% for 5-6½ minutes. Cool in the dish before cutting into squares.

COCONUT ALMOND MACAROONS

100%, 70%...6 minutes
Makes 12

Take care not to overcook these delicate biscuits.

125 g (4 oz) desiccated coconut
60 g (2 oz) sugar
2 egg whites (large eggs)
45 ml (3 tbsp) plain flour
generous pinch of baking powder
few drops of almond essence
few drops of vanilla essence
2.5 ml (½ tsp) finely grated lemon rind
maraschino cherries or pecan nuts to decorate

Combine coconut, 30 g (1 oz) sugar and 1 egg white. Mix well and microwave on 100% for 2 minutes, stirring twice. Mix in the flour, baking powder, almond and vanilla essence and lemon rind. Beat remaining egg white to soft peaks, then gradually beat in remaining sugar. Fold into the coconut mixture. Spoon into 12 paper baking cups and bake 6 at a time in a microwave muffin pan. Microwave on 70% for 1½-2 minutes. Cool in the paper cups on a wire rack. Top with quarter maraschino cherry or half a pecan nut if desired.

APRICOT SESAME BARS

100%...8 minutes
Makes 16

100 g (3½ oz) butter or margarine
125 g (4 oz) golden syrup
75 g (2½ oz) dried apricots, finely chopped
grated rind and juice of 1 orange
175 g (6 oz) plain flour
7.5 ml (1½ tsp) baking powder
2.5 ml (½ tsp) salt
30 ml (2 tbsp) sesame seeds, toasted
2 eggs
few drops of vanilla essence
30 ml (2 tbsp) smooth apricot jam
30 ml (2 tbsp) sesame seeds, toasted

Place butter in a large microwave bowl. Microwave on 100% for 45 seconds, then stir to melt. Add golden syrup, apricots, orange rind and juice. Microwave for 2 minutes. Stir well. Combine flour, baking powder, salt and sesame seeds, add to the apricot mixture and beat well. Mix in the beaten eggs and vanilla. Turn into a greased 23-cm (9-in) square baking dish and microwave on 100% for 4-5 minutes. The centre will still be moist. Do not overcook, as the mixture will firm during standing time. Let cool. Microwave apricot jam for 20 seconds, then brush over the surface. Sprinkle with toasted sesame seeds. To serve, cut into bars.

CARAMEL SPICE SHORTBREAD

100%, 70%...7 minutes
plus Combination baking
Makes 12 wedges

SHORTBREAD
200 g (7 oz) plain flour
5 ml (1 tsp) baking powder
pinch of salt
2.5 ml (½ tsp) cinnamon
generous pinch of ground nutmeg
pinch of allspice
150 g (5 oz) butter, softened
45 g (1½ oz) icing sugar

TOPPING
170 ml (5½ fl oz) condensed milk
45 g (1½ oz) butter
60 g (2 oz) caster sugar
15 ml (1 tbsp) golden syrup
few drops of vanilla essence
75 g (2½ oz) plain chocolate

To make the shortbread, combine flour, baking powder, salt and spices. Cream butter and sugar until well mixed. Gradually mix in the dry ingredients. Press the mixture into a greased and lined, 18-cm (7-in) pie plate. Bake according to instructions below. Cool in the dish.

For the topping, combine condensed milk, butter, caster sugar and golden syrup. Microwave on 100% for 3 minutes, then beat very well. Stir in vanilla and microwave for 1-2 minutes more, or until very thick and bubbly. Let cool a few minutes before spreading over the shortbread. Cool. Microwave chocolate on 70% for 1½-2 minutes, then spread over the caramel. Cool before cutting into wedges.

BROTHER
Hi-Speed at 160 °C for 8-9 minutes.

PEANUT & COFFEE BISCUITS

70%...6 minutes
Makes about 36

125 g (4 oz) peanut butter
100 g (3½ oz) margarine
100 g (3½ oz) sugar
60 g (2 oz) soft brown sugar
2 eggs
10 ml (2 tsp) instant coffee granules
10 ml (2 tsp) boiling water
200 g (7 oz) plain flour
2.5 ml (½ tsp) bicarbonate of soda
pinch of salt
45 g (1½ oz) salted peanuts, finely chopped

Beat peanut butter, margarine, sugar and brown sugar very well. Beat in the eggs. Dissolve coffee in boiling water and beat into mixture. Sift the dry ingredients together and add to the creamed mixture. Mix in peanuts. Refrigerate dough for 1 hour. Line or grease a microwave baking sheet. Form mixture into large walnut-sized balls, then flatten with a fork. Arrange 12 biscuits at a time around the outside of the baking sheet. Microwave on 70% for 1½-2 minutes. Remove from baking sheet and cool on a wire rack. Repeat until mixture has been used up.

GINGER CRUNCH BISCUITS

100%, 30%...19 minutes
Makes about 36

100 g (3½ oz) margarine
60 ml (4 tbsp) golden syrup
100 g (3½ oz) sugar
5 ml (1 tsp) bicarbonate of soda
250 g (9 oz) plain flour
15 ml (1 tbsp) ground ginger
water

ICING
100 g (3½ oz) icing sugar
generous pinch of ground ginger
lemon juice
preserved ginger

Microwave margarine in a bowl on 30% for about 40 seconds to make it very soft. Add syrup, sugar and bicarbonate of soda, beat very well. Sift flour and ginger and work into the mixture, adding enough water to make a dough. Roll dough out thinly, prick dough with a skewer. Using a fluted cutter, cut out 5-cm (2-in) diameter biscuits. Place biscuits in a circle on a greased microwave baking sheet. Microwave on 100% for 2½-3 minutes. Lift biscuits onto a wire rack to cool. Repeat with more dough. When cool, ice the biscuits by drizzling a little of the icing onto the biscuit, top with a piece of preserved ginger.

To make the icing, sift icing sugar and ginger, add sufficient lemon juice to form a runny consistency.

DOUBLE CHOCOLATE CUP CAKES

100%...4 minutes
Makes 6

So easy and so good, these individual cup cakes bake in just 2 minutes.

75 g (2½ oz) plain flour
100 g (3½ oz) sugar
45 ml (3 tbsp) cocoa powder
5 ml (1 tsp) baking powder
pinch of salt
15 ml (1 tbsp) desiccated coconut
75 ml (2½ fl oz) water
1 egg
60 ml (4 tbsp) oil
few drops of vanilla essence
60 g (2 oz) chocolate chips

Combine flour, sugar, cocoa, baking powder, salt and coconut in a mixing bowl. Combine water, egg, oil and vanilla and add to dry ingredients. Beat on low speed to moisten, then on medium speed until mixture is smooth. Stir in chocolate chips and spoon into greased custard cups. Microwave 3 at a time on 100% for 2 minutes, or until a wooden skewer comes out clean. Allow cakes to stand while microwaving remaining 3, then loosen edges and turn cakes out. Serve warm or cool, topped with whipped cream. Store in an airtight container.

Madeleines

MADELEINES

100%...4 minutes
Makes 8

125 g (4 oz) butter, softened
125 g (4 oz) caster sugar
2 extra large eggs
few drops of vanilla essence
125 g (4 oz) plain flour
5 ml (1 tsp) baking powder
2.5 ml (½ tsp) salt
100 g (3½ oz) smooth apricot jam
2 drops almond essence
75 g (2½ oz) desiccated coconut, toasted
glacé cherries to decorate

Line the base of 8 ordinary paper drinking cups with rounds of waxed paper and spray the insides of the cups with non-stick coating. Combine butter, sugar, eggs, vanilla, flour, baking powder and salt and beat until smooth. Divide the mixture between the prepared cups and arrange 4 in a circular pattern in the microwave oven. Microwave on 100% for 1½-2 minutes, or until well risen but still moist on top. Remove from the oven, and repeat with remaining paper cups. Allow to stand for 3-4 minutes, then carefully turn out and cool on a wire rack. Trim bases evenly. Microwave apricot jam and almond essence for 45 seconds, or until melted. Mix well, then brush the sides and top of each madeleine. Roll in toasted coconut to coat well. Top each with half a cherry. Store in an airtight container.

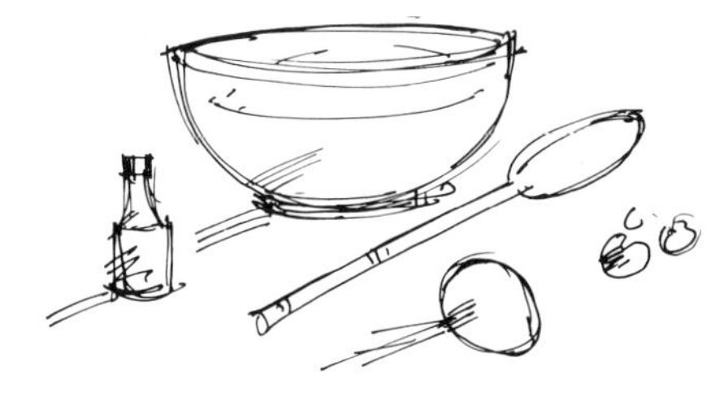

TEA CAKES

Italian Slice

CAKES are really the aristocrats of foods, and a fresh, home-made cake is a treat for family and friends. Nowadays many good cooks just do not have time to whip up and bake cakes from scratch. The microwave oven will shorten the baking time without losing any of the delicious flavour that everyone enjoys. Microwave cakes rise high and have an airy texture, although those baked on microwave energy alone do not brown. This is not important if the cake is to be iced or served with a topping. In this chapter we have included recipes for plain and rich cakes, plus some for cakes baked on combination cooking; these look very similar to conventional ones, but bake in much less time.

ITALIAN SLICE

100%... 30 seconds
Serves 8-10

1 × Madeira cake without cherries, baked (page 55)
FILLING
150 g (5 oz) ricotta cheese
125 g (4 oz) plain chocolate, chopped
100 g (3½ oz) sugar
few drops of vanilla essence
90 ml (3 fl oz) Amaretto liqueur
TOPPING
200 g (7 oz) caster sugar
15 g (½ oz) cocoa powder, sifted
15 g (½ oz) butter
45-60 ml (3-4 tbsp) boiling water
45 ml (3 tbsp) coarsely chopped walnuts

Place the cake in the freezer for 1 hour, then slice horizontally in three.

To make the filling, combine all the ingredients, except liqueur. Reserve about 30 g (1 oz) of the filling and spread the remainder on two of the layers. Reassemble the cake, drizzle the liqueur over the top of the cake.

To make the topping, combine caster sugar and cocoa powder. Microwave butter on 100% for 30 seconds, add to the sugar mixture, adding sufficient water to give a thick pouring consistency. Pour over the cake, allowing the mixture to drizzle down over the sides. Dollop remaining cheese mixture down the middle of the icing. Sprinkle with walnuts. Chill well before serving.

SOURED CREAM SPICE CAKE

100%... 10 minutes
Makes 1 × 23cm (9-in) cake

175 g (6 oz) plain flour
300 g (11 oz) caster sugar
75 g (2½ oz) butter
250 ml (8 fl oz) soured cream
1 egg
2.5 ml (½ tsp) ground nutmeg
generous pinch of ground cloves
2.5 ml (½ tsp) cinnamon
2.5 ml (½ tsp) ground allspice
2.5 ml (½ tsp) bicarbonate or soda
2.5 ml (½ tsp) ground nutmeg
45 g (1½ oz) hazelnuts, chopped

Combine flour, brown sugar and butter until crumbly. Set aside 175 g (6 oz) of the mixture. Mix together soured cream, egg, spices and bicarbonate of soda and stir into remaining crumb mixture until moistened. Spread evenly in a round greased or sprayed 23-cm (9-in) dish. Sprinkle with reserved crumb mixture and nuts. Microwave on 100% for 8-10 minutes, or until a cocktail stick inserted near the centre comes out clean. Cool in dish, then turn out and slice.

CHOCOLATE CARROT & CASHEW CAKE

Combination baking
Makes 1 × 20-cm (8-in) cake

125 g (4 oz) self-raising flour
15 g (½ oz) cocoa powder
2.5 ml (½ tsp) bicarbonate of soda
100 g (3½ oz) caster sugar
2.5 ml (½ tsp) cinnamon
generous pinch of ground nutmeg
pinch of ground cloves
1 tart apple, peeled and grated
2 extra large eggs
45 g (1½ oz) cashew nuts, coarsely chopped
150 g (5 oz) grated carrot
125 ml (4 fl oz) oil
cream cheese icing (page 92)

Sift flour, cocoa, bicarbonate of soda, sugar and spices into a mixing bowl. Add grated apple, eggs, nuts, carrot and oil. Mix until well moistened, then pour into a greased and lined, deep 20-cm (8-in) baking tin. Bake according to instructions given below or until skewer inserted in the centre comes out clean. Cool in the pan for a few minutes, then turn out and cool on a wire rack. Ice with cream cheese icing.

BROTHER
Hi-Speed at 250 °C for 12-14 minutes.

ORANGE SPICE CAKE

Combination baking
Makes 1 × 20-cm (8-in) square cake

175 g (6 oz) butter or margarine
15 ml (1 tbsp) grated orange rind
150 g (5 oz) sugar
3 eggs, separated
150 g (5 oz) orange marmalade
60 g (2 oz) mixed peel
300 g (11 oz) plain flour
15 ml (1 tbsp) baking powder
5 ml (1 tsp) salt
2.5 ml (½ tsp) cinnamon
2.5 ml (½ tsp) ground nutmeg
pinch of ground cloves
125 ml (4 fl oz) milk
60 ml (4 tbsp) orange juice
ICING
60 g (2 oz) butter
10 ml (2 tsp) grated orange rind
150 g (5 oz) icing sugar
15 ml (1 tbsp) orange juice
orange twists to decorate

Beat butter, orange rind, sugar and egg yolks with an electric mixer until light and fluffy. Mix in marmalade and peel. Sift flour with baking powder, salt and spices and add to the mixture alternately with the milk and orange juice. Beat egg whites until firm and fold into the cake mixture.

Turn into a greased and lined, deep 20-cm (8-in) square cake pan. Bake according to instructions below. Turn out onto a wire rack to cool, then spread with icing.

To make the icing, cream butter and orange rind, gradually beat in sifted icing sugar and enough orange juice to make a spreading consistency.

BROTHER
Hi-Speed at 160 °C for 28-35 minutes.

ALMOND CHOCOLATE ROULADE

100%, 50%... 11 minutes
Serves 8-10

This roulade requires a 30-cm (12-in) square microwave baking dish and a microwave oven with a large interior capacity so that the cake will bake evenly.

10 ml (2 tsp) melted butter
100 g (3½ oz) flaked almonds, toasted
2.5 ml (½ tsp) baking powder
4 eggs, separated
45 g (1½ oz) icing sugar
few drops of vanilla essence
few drops of almond essence
FILLING
100 g (3½ oz) plain chocolate
100 g (3½ oz) milk chocolate
250 ml (8 fl oz) single cream
15 ml (1 tbsp) rum

Line the baking pan with two overlapping layers of waxed paper so that they extend over the edges, and brush well with the melted butter. Place the almonds in a food processor and process until finely ground. Stir in baking powder and set aside. Beat egg yolks with icing sugar, vanilla and almond essence until light. Stir in almond mixture. Beat egg whites to stiff peaks and gently fold into the egg yolk mixture. Spread in prepared pan. Elevate the pan in the microwave oven and microwave on 100% for 5-7 minutes, or until just set. Remove from oven, stand for 2 minutes. Using paper handles, remove roulade from pan and place on a wire rack. Cover with a damp towel and let cool completely. When ready to assemble, turn roulade over onto a piece of waxed paper and peel off backing paper. Trim the edges, then spread with filling.

To make the filling, break up chocolate and place in a bowl. Microwave on 50% for 3-4 minutes, or until melted. Mix in the cream and rum and cool. Then beat until smooth. Spread mixture on the roulade and roll up Swiss roll fashion. Chill until needed. Dust with icing sugar if desired and cut into slices to serve.

Lemon Jelly Cake

LEMON JELLY CAKE

100%, 50%... 12 minutes
Makes 1 × 20-cm (8-in) square cake

125 g (4 oz) plain flour
125 g (4 oz) sugar
7.5 ml (1½ tsp) baking powder
2.5 ml (½ tsp) salt
75 g (2½ oz) butter or margarine, softened
few drops of vanilla essence
75 ml (2½ fl oz) milk
2 large eggs
2 egg whites
10 ml (2 tsp) grated lemon rind
TOPPING
200 ml (6½ fl oz) water
½ × 90 g (3 oz) packet lemon jelly

Combine flour, sugar, baking powder and salt in a mixing bowl. Add butter or margarine. Combine vanilla, milk, eggs and egg whites, and lemon rind and add to dry ingredients. Mix at low speed with an electric mixer until mixture is moistened. Beat at medium speed for about 2 minutes or until mixture is smooth. Turn mixture into a greased 20-cm (8-in) square baking dish. Smooth the top and microwave on 50% for 6 minutes, then increase the power to 100% and microwave for 1-3 minutes more. The cake should appear slightly moist on top. Allow to stand for about 10 minutes.

While cake is standing, prepare the topping. Microwave water on 100% for about 3 minutes, or until boiling. Stir in lemon jelly, mixing well to dissolve. Pierce cake all over with a wooden skewer and gently pour hot jelly mixture over the cake. Cool, then chill well. Serve topped with whipped cream or fluffy icing (page 91).

VARIATION

☐ Substitute strawberry or lime jelly for the lemon.

TANGERINE YOGHURT CAKE

100%...7 minutes
Makes 1 large ring cake

175 g (6 oz) self-raising flour
90 g (3 oz) caster sugar
100 g (3½ oz) margarine or butter, softened
15 ml (1 tbsp) grated tangerine rind
2 large eggs
150 ml (5 fl oz) tangerine-flavoured yoghurt
few drops of vanilla essence

Combine all ingredients in a mixing bowl and beat on low speed to moisten. Then beat on medium speed for about 2 minutes, or until mixture is smooth. Grease a 1-litre (1¾-pint) ring pan and line the bottom with a ring of greaseproof or waxed paper. Turn in the cake mixture, smooth the top and microwave on 100% for 5-7 minutes, or until cake is well risen. The cake should be firm to the touch, but still moist on top. Allow to cool in the pan before turning out. If desired, glaze with orange glaze (page 90) or ice with cream cheese icing (page 92).

DATE & BEER RING

70%...12 minutes
Makes 1 × 25-cm (10-in) ring cake

200 g (7 oz) soft brown sugar
125 g (4 oz) butter
2 eggs
200 g (7 oz) plain flour
5 ml (1 tsp) mixed spice
5 ml (1 tsp) bicarbonate of soda
60 g (2 oz) pecan nuts, chopped
150 g (5 oz) dates, chopped
200 ml (6½ fl oz) beer

Cream sugar and butter together until light and fluffy. Beat in eggs one at a time. Sift flour, mixed spice and bicarbonate of soda. Combine nuts and dates and add 30 ml (2 tbsp) of the sifted flour, toss to coat fruit with flour. Mix flour into the creamed mixture, alternately with the beer. Stir in date mixture. Turn mixture into a well-greased or sprayed 25-cm (10-in) fluted ring pan. Microwave on 70% for 10-12 minutes. Stand on a flat surface until cool. Turn cake onto a wire rack and dust lightly with icing sugar.

Coffee & Cream Gateau

COFFEE & CREAM GATEAU

100%, 50%...6 minutes
Makes 1 × 20-cm (8-in) cake

1 × recipe microwave hot water sponge, baked (page 93)
SYRUP
45 g (1½ oz) sugar
45 ml (3 tbsp) water
45 ml (3 tbsp) dark rum
45 ml (3 tbsp) Grand Marnier
CRÈME PÂTISSIÈRE FILLING
250 ml (8 fl oz) milk
3 egg yolks
75 g (2½ oz) caster sugar
few drops of vanilla essence
15 g (½ oz) cornflour
30 ml (2 tbsp) boiling water
10 ml (2 tsp) instant coffee granules
250 ml (8 fl oz) whipping cream
TO DECORATE
150 ml (5 fl oz) whipping cream
fruit or chocolate

While the cake is cooling make the syrup: combine sugar and water in a jug, microwave on 100% for 2 minutes, stirring once during cooking time. Cool slightly, then add the rum and Grand Marnier, cool.

To make the filling: microwave milk on 100% for 2 minutes. Beat yolks, sugar and vanilla until thick and pale, then mix in the cornflour. Pour boiling milk onto this mixture, stirring constantly. Microwave for 2 minutes on 50%, stirring every minute. Combine water and coffee granules, stir into custard mixture. Place a piece of greaseproof paper directly on top of the mixture to prevent a skin from forming. Allow to cool. Whip cream until peaking consistency, fold into cooled mixture.

To assemble: Using a serrated knife, cut a circle 15 mm (¾ in) from the edge of the cake. Using a spatula carefully lift off the 'lid', set aside. Remove cake centre to approximately half the depth of the cake to form a cavity. Brush the syrup mixture over the sides and base of the cavity. Pile filling in the centre, cover filling with the 'lid'. Brush any remaining syrup on the lid. Chill well.

To serve, decorate with rosettes of whipped cream, and fruit or chocolate.

Front *Blueberry Lemon Cake*; back *Easy Soured Cream Chocolate Cake*

EASY SOURED CREAM CHOCOLATE CAKE

100%... 13 minutes
Makes 1 large ring cake

Use a cake mix and make something really special.

1 packet chocolate cake mix
30 g (1 oz) hazelnuts, toasted and finely ground
4 eggs
250 ml (8 fl oz) soured cream
185 ml (6 fl oz) oil
100 g (3½ oz) caster sugar

Combine cake mix with hazelnuts, mixing well. Mix together the eggs, soured cream, oil and sugar and add to the dry ingredients. Blend on low speed of an electric mixer for 1 minute to moisten. Increase speed to medium and beat for 3 minutes. Turn into a large ring pan and microwave on 100% for 9-13 minutes, or until a skewer inserted near the centre comes out clean. Stand for 10 minutes, then turn out and cool on a wire rack. Ice as desired or dust with icing sugar.

CHOCOLATE ORANGE PECAN CAKE

100%... 1 minute
plus Combination baking
Makes 1 × 20-cm (8-in) cake

60 g (2 oz) plain chocolate, broken up
60 g (2 oz) butter
60 ml (4 tbsp) water
175 g (6 oz) self-raising flour
15 g (½ oz) cocoa powder
200 g (7 oz) caster sugar
1 egg, beaten
15 ml (1 tbsp) grated orange rind
few drops of vanilla essence
60 ml (4 tbsp) orange juice
60 ml (4 tbsp) milk
45 g (1½ oz) pecan nuts, finely chopped

Microwave chocolate and butter on 100% for 1 minute. Stir until smooth. Add water, sifted flour, cocoa powder, caster sugar, egg, orange rind, vanilla, orange juice and milk. Beat until smooth, then stir in nuts. Turn into a deep, greased and lined 20-cm (8-in) round cake tin and bake according to instructions below. Cool in the tin for 5 minutes, then turn out onto a wire rack to cool. When cold, ice with chocolate orange icing (page 90) if desired.

BROTHER
Hi-Speed at 200 °C for 13-18 minutes.

CREAM CHEESE PECAN CAKE

100%... 12 minutes
Makes 1 large ring cake

1 packet lemon cake mix
250 g low-fat soft cheese
4 eggs
150 g (5 oz) butter, softened
60 ml (4 tbsp) water
few drops of vanilla essence
45 g (1½ oz) pecan nuts, finely chopped
GLAZE
125 g (4 oz) icing sugar, sifted
30 ml (2 tbsp) hot water
30 ml (2 tbsp) lemon juice
few drops of vanilla essence
pinch of salt

Place cake mix in a mixing bowl. Add cottage cheese, eggs, butter, water and vanilla and beat on low speed for 1 minute. Increase speed to medium and beat for 3 minutes. Fold in nuts and turn into a large microwave ring pan. Microwave on 100% for 8-12 minutes, or until a skewer inserted near the centre comes out clean. Stand for 10 minutes before turning out to cool. When cool drizzle with the glaze.

To make the glaze, combine icing sugar, water, lemon juice, vanilla and salt. Mix well and spoon over the cake.

BLUEBERRY & LEMON CAKE

70%... 18 minutes
Makes 1 × 20-cm (8-in) layer cake

The combination of flavours is delicious – and fresh blueberries are sometimes available in large supermarkets.

4 eggs
300 g (11 oz) sugar
200 g (7 oz) plain flour, sifted
10 ml (2 tsp) baking powder
375 ml (12 fl oz) whipping cream
few drops of vanilla essence
generous pinch of salt
100 g (3½ oz) walnuts, finely ground
150 g (5 oz) fresh or frozen blueberries
fresh blueberries and lemon leaves (optional) for decoration
FILLING
125 g (4 oz) butter, softened
250 g (9 oz) icing sugar, sifted
15 ml (1 tbsp) lemon juice
10 ml (2 tsp) grated lemon rind
few drops of vanilla essence
blueberries and citrus fruit leaves (if available) to garnish
2 egg yolks
extra icing sugar

Beat eggs until thick. Beat in sugar a little at a time and mix until light and fluffy. Sift flour and baking powder together and set aside. Beat cream, vanilla and salt to stiff peaks and fold into the butter mixture alternating with the flour mixture and nuts. Divide the mixture between three 20-cm (8-in) greased and lined baking dishes. Sprinkle each layer with a third of the blueberries. Microwave each layer on 70% for 4-6 minutes or until skewer inserted in centre comes out clean. Stand for 5 minutes, then turn out onto wire racks to cool.

To prepare filling, beat butter, sugar, lemon juice and rind and vanilla until light and fluffy. Beat in egg yolks, one at a time, beating well after each addition.

When cake has cooled, place 1 layer on a serving plate, spread with half the filling. Repeat with second layer and top with the last layer. Sprinkle the top of the cake with icing sugar and garnish with blueberries and lemon leaves.

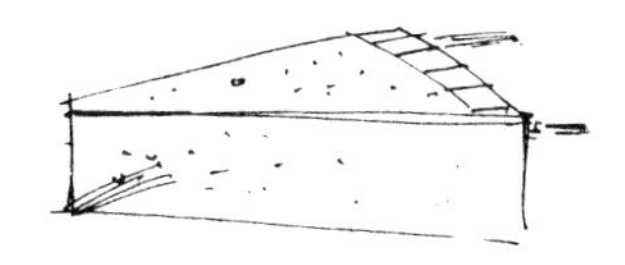

Southern Coffee Cake

SOUTHERN COFFEE CAKE

70%... 14 minutes
Makes 1 × 23-cm (9-in) layer cake

125 g (4 oz) butter
150 g (5 oz) icing sugar
3 eggs
5 ml (1 tsp) instant coffee powder
75 ml (2½ fl oz) cold black coffee
75 ml (2½ fl oz) buttermilk
250 g (8 oz) plain flour
10 ml (2 tsp) baking powder
2.5 ml (½ tsp) bicarbonate of soda
coffee buttercream (page 91)
few coffee beans soaked in brandy overnight to decorate

Cream butter and sugar together until light and fluffy. Beat in eggs one at a time, beating well after each addition. Dissolve coffee powder in coffee, then beat into creamed mixture. Beat in buttermilk. Sift dry ingredients together, mix quickly into creamed mixture. Turn mixture into 2 well-greased 23-cm (9-in) straight-sided dishes. Microwave one at a time on 70% for 6-7 minutes. Cool on a flat surface, then turn out onto a wire rack. Spread both layers with a little coffee buttercream, sandwich together, then spread remaining icing around the sides. Decorate with coffee beans.

CREAM CHEESE BUTTER RING

70%... 17 minutes
Makes 1 × 23-cm (9-in) ring cake

200 g (7 oz) butter
225 g (8 oz) caster sugar
3 eggs
200 g (7 oz) fresh cream cheese
few drops of vanilla essence
225 g (8 oz) plain flour
scant 10 ml (2 tsp) baking powder
200 g (7 oz) dates, chopped
icing sugar

Cream butter and sugar well, add eggs one at a time and beat until light. Beat in cream cheese and vanilla. Sift flour and baking powder together, add 30 ml (2 tbsp) to the chopped dates, toss to coat dates with flour. Beat flour mixture into creamed mixture and then mix in the dates. Turn into a well-oiled or sprayed 23-cm (9-in) ring pan. Microwave on 70% for 14-17 minutes. Allow to stand on a flat surface until cool. Turn out and dust generously with sifted icing sugar.

ORANGE LIQUEUR SPONGE

100%, 50%... 24 minutes
Makes 1 × 25-cm (10-in) ring cake

1 packet vanilla cake mix
90 g (3 oz) packet vanilla instant pudding
4 eggs
60 ml (4 tbsp) oil
60 ml (4 tbsp) orange liqueur
185 ml (6 fl oz) orange juice
60 ml (4 tbsp) water
strips of orange rind to decorate

ICING
125 g (4 oz) icing sugar, sifted
15 ml (1 tbsp) orange juice
15 ml (1 tbsp) water
15 ml (1 tbsp) orange liqueur
15 ml (1 tbsp) golden syrup

Grease or spray a 25-cm (10-in) ring pan. Place the cake ingredients, except the orange rind, in a mixing bowl. Beat for 3-4 minutes using an electric mixer. Pour mixture into the pan. Microwave cake on 100% for 4 minutes. Reduce power to 50% and microwave for 18-20 minutes, or until a skewer inserted into the centre comes out clean. Allow cake to stand for about 15 minutes before turning out onto a wire rack.

To make the icing, combine all the ingredients in a bowl, beat until smooth. Drizzle over cooled cake and decorate with strips of orange rind.

CHERRY MADEIRA CAKE

Combination baking
Makes 1 loaf

150 g (5 oz) butter or margarine
150 g (5 oz) caster sugar
3 eggs
5 ml (1 tsp) grated lemon rind
20 ml (4 tsp) milk
200 g (7 oz) plain flour
5 ml (1 tsp) baking powder
generous pinch of salt
45 g (1½ oz) glacé cherries, cut up

Cream butter and sugar together very well. Add eggs one at a time, beating well after each addition. Add lemon rind and milk. Sift together the dry ingredients and add 15 ml (1 tbsp) to cherries, tossing to coat them with flour. Beat remaining flour into creamed mixture, then stir in the cherries. Pour into a greased and lined 23 × 13 cm loaf tin. Bake according to instructions below. Allow to cool in tin before turning out.

BROTHER
Hi-Speed at 210 °C for 10 minutes, then Turbo at 250 °C for 4 minutes.

Wholemeal Fig Cake

WHOLEMEAL FIG CAKE

70%... 11 minutes
Makes 1 × 20-cm (8-in) cake

150 g (5 oz) butter or margarine
125 g (4 oz) soft brown sugar
3 eggs
90 g (3 oz) wholemeal flour
45 g (1½ oz) bran
60 g (2 oz) self-raising flour
12.5 ml (2½ tsp) baking powder
1 lemon
200 g (7 oz) dried figs, chopped
60 g (2 oz) carrot, grated
TO DECORATE
100 g (3½ oz) caramel sugar
zest of 1 lemon

Cream butter and sugar until light and fluffy. Add eggs one at a time, beating well after each addition. Mix in wholemeal flour and bran, then add sifted self-raising flour and baking powder. Grate the rind of the lemon and add to the mixture. Peel the lemon and remove segments, chop and add to mixture. Stir in figs and carrot. Turn into a greased 20-cm (8-in) cake dish. Microwave on 70% for 9-11 minutes. Allow to cool for 15 minutes on a flat surface before removing the cake from the dish. Sprinkle with sugar and lemon zest.

BLACK FOREST CAKE

100%, 70%...10 minutes
Makes 1 × 20-cm (8-in) cake

125 g (4 oz) margarine
200 g (7 oz) caster sugar
3 eggs
few drops of almond essence
250 g (9 oz) self-raising flour
30 g (1 oz) cocoa powder
30 g (1 oz) ground almonds
generous pinch of baking powder
salt
100 ml (3½ fl oz) natural yoghurt
60 ml (4 tbsp) Kirsch or Maraschino
400 ml (13 fl oz) whipping cream, stiffly beaten
400 g (14 oz) cherry pie filling
2 large chocolate flaky bars
maraschino cherries
10 ml (2 tsp) icing sugar

Cream margarine and sugar until light and fluffy, add eggs and almond essence, beat well. Sift the flour, cocoa, ground almonds, baking powder and salt. Add about one-third to the creamed mixture and beat well. Add one-third of the yoghurt and beat well. Repeat until dry ingredients and yoghurt have been used up. Line the base of a deep 20-cm (8-in) dish with parchment paper, spray or grease the sides. Pour in the cake mixture, microwave on 70% for 7 minutes, then increase power level to 100% for 2-3 minutes. Allow to stand for at least 10 minutes before removing from the pan. Turn onto a wire rack and allow to cool.

Split the cake into 3 layers. Sprinkle each layer with Kirsch or Maraschino. Using a piping bag fitted with a medium-sized star nozzle, pipe a circle of cream around the outside of the bottom layer. Fill with cherry pie filling. Place a second layer of cake on top of the cherries and spread with cream, then place the third layer on top. Cover the top and sides of the cake with cream. Pipe generous swirls of cream on the top. Reserve a few large bits of the flaky bar for decoration, chop the rest roughly. Press chocolate bits onto the sides of the cake and in the middle on the top. Place a cherry on top of each rosette of cream and add a piece of the reserved chocolate. Sprinkle a little icing sugar over the centre.

Year-Round Fruit Cake

YEAR-ROUND FRUIT CAKE

100%, 30%...57 minutes
Makes 1 × 20-cm (8-in) cake

150 g (5 oz) sultanas
150 g (5 oz) currants
150 g (5 oz) raisins
75 g (2½ oz) mixed peel
250 ml (8 fl oz) cold tea (citrus-flavoured is also good)
75 g (2½ oz) sugar
125 g (4 oz) butter or margarine
5 ml (1 tsp) bicarbonate of soda
60 g (2 oz) glacé cherries, cut up
2 eggs, lightly beaten
250 g (9 oz) plain flour
5 ml (1 tsp) baking powder
125 ml (4 fl oz) brandy or sherry

Place fruit, tea, sugar, and butter into a large bowl. Microwave on 100% for 7 minutes, stirring at least twice during the cooking time. Stir in bicarbonate of soda and cherries and allow to cool completely. Stir in the remaining ingredients, turn mixture into a 20-cm (8-in) lined and greased straight-sided dish. Cover with vented plastic wrap. Microwave on 30% for 40-50 minutes. Allow cake to cool on a flat surface before turning out onto a wire rack. Wrap tightly in foil or plastic wrap to store. Mature with extra brandy if desired.

BOSTON CREAM CAKE

100%, 50%... 18 minutes
Makes 1 × 20-cm (8-in) layer cake

2 eggs
200 g (7 oz) sugar
125 g (4 oz) plain flour
5 ml (1 tsp) baking powder
125 ml (4 fl oz) milk
30 g (1 oz) butter
45 ml (3 tbsp) apricot jam

FILLING
75 g (2½ oz) sugar
15 g (½ oz) plain flour
20 ml (4 tsp) cornflour
pinch of salt
300 ml (10 fl oz) milk
2 egg yolks, beaten
15 g (½ oz) butter
15 ml (1 tbsp) apricot liqueur or brandy
few drops of vanilla essence

GLAZE
30 g (1 oz) plain chocolate
15 g (½ oz) butter
175 g (6 oz) icing sugar
few drops of vanilla essence
hot water
10 ml (2 tsp) milk

For the sponge, beat eggs very well with an electric mixer, then gradually add the sugar, beating until the mixture is thick and pale and the sugar almost dissolved. Combine flour and baking powder and add to egg mixture, stirring until just blended. Place milk in a jug, add butter and microwave on 100% for 20-30 seconds, just to melt butter. Add milk to cake mixture, stirring until smooth. Turn into a greased and lined 20 cm (8-in) round baking dish and microwave on 50% for 7-8 minutes, then on 100% for 1½-2 minutes until just cooked. Cool in the dish for about 10 minutes, then turn out onto a wire rack to cool completely.

To make the filling, combine sugar, flour, cornflour and salt in a 1-litre (1¾-pint) bowl. Gradually stir in milk, mixing well. Microwave on 100% for 4 minutes, stirring every minute. Microwave for 1 minute more. Gradually stir a small amount of the milk mixture into beaten egg yolks, then return to the bowl, mixing well. Microwave on 100% for 45 seconds, stirring every 15 seconds. Add remaining ingredients, stir until butter melts. Cover surface with greaseproof paper and cool without stirring. Chill very well.

For the glaze, place chocolate and butter in a jug, microwave on 100% for 1½-2 minutes or until the chocolate has melted. Stir in 100 g (3½ oz) of the icing sugar and the vanilla, then 10 ml (2 tsp) hot water. Add a further 15-30 ml (1-2 tbsp) hot water, a little at a time, and blend well, until mixture is of a pouring consistency. For the white icing, combine remaining 75 g (2½ oz) icing sugar and 10 ml (2 tsp) milk to make a drizzling consistency.

To assemble: slice cake horizontally into two layers and spread bottom layer with apricot jam. Place on a serving plate. Top with the custard filling, spreading to within 1 cm (½ in) of the edges. Place remaining cake half on top. Pour over chocolate glaze and spread evenly. Drizzle white icing in a spiral pattern, then quickly draw a sharp knife from the centre to the edge of the cake.

Boston Cream Cake

CHERRY, PECAN & WHISKY CAKE

100%...8 minutes
plus Convection baking
Makes 1 × 23-cm (9-in) layer cake

400 g (14 oz) sugar
300 g (11 oz) butter or margarine
few drops of vanilla essence
425 g (15 oz) plain flour
25 ml (5 tsp) baking powder
7.5 ml (1½ tsp) salt
375 ml (12 fl oz) milk
8 egg whites, stiffly beaten

FILLING
125 g (4 oz) butter or margarine
200 g (7 oz) caster sugar
75 ml (2½ fl oz) whisky
75 ml (2½ fl oz) water
9 egg yolks, lightly beaten
150 g (5 oz) raisins, chopped
100 g (3½ oz) pecans, finely chopped
75 g (2½ oz) maraschino cherries, drained and chopped
45 g (1½ oz) desiccated coconut
few drops of vanilla essence
fluffy icing (page 91)

First make the filling by microwaving butter on 100% for 1 minute. Stir in sugar, whisky and water and microwave for 3-4 minutes, or until just boiling. Stir to dissolve sugar. Mix about half the hot mixture into the egg yolks, then return to the hot mixture.

Microwave for 3 minutes or until thickened, stirring every minute. Remove from oven, add raisins, pecans, cherries and coconut. Stir in vanilla, cover and cool to room temperature.

To make the cake, combine sugar, butter and vanilla and beat with an electric mixer until light and fluffy. Sift flour, baking powder and salt and add to the butter mixture alternately with the milk, beating well after each addition. Fold in the egg whites.

Divide batter among 3 greased, lined and floured, 23-cm (9-in) cake tins. Bake on convection at 190 °C (375 °F) for about 20 minutes. Cool layers in tins for 10 minutes, then turn out onto a wire rack to cool.

To assemble the cake, place one layer on a serving plate, top with a third of the filling. Repeat with remaining layers, ending with last third of the filling. Pipe or ice sides and around top edges of the cake with Fluffy icing.

Cherry, Pecan & Whisky Cake

BANANA CAKE

100%, 50%...14 minutes
Makes 1 × 25-cm (10-in) ring cake

125 g (4 oz) butter, softened
275 g (10 oz) sugar
2 eggs
225 g (8 oz) bananas, mashed
few drops of almond essence
275 g (10 oz) plain flour
2.5 ml (½ tsp) baking powder
2.5 ml (½ tsp) bicarbonate of soda
pinch of salt
60 ml (4 tbsp) natural yoghurt
banana fudge icing (page 91)

Grease a 25-cm (10-in) ring pan. Cream butter and sugar until light and fluffy. Beat in eggs one at a time. Add banana and almond essence. Sift dry ingredients together. Add about a third of the dry ingredients to banana mixture, beat to combine. Add a third of the yoghurt and beat. Continue until all the ingredients have been combined. Pour mixture into ring pan. Microwave on 50% for 12 minutes, increase power to 100% and microwave for a further 1-2 minutes. Allow cake to stand in pan for about 15 minutes before turning out onto a wire rack. Cool completely before icing with banana fudge icing.

Carrot Cake

CARROT CAKE

100%...7 minutes
Makes 1 × 25-cm (10-in) ring cake

125 ml (4 fl oz) oil
150 g (5 oz) soft brown sugar
2 eggs
2.5 ml (½ tsp) bicarbonate of soda
few drops of vanilla essence
150 g (5 oz) self-raising flour
2.5 ml (½ tsp) mixed spice
5 ml (1 tsp) cinnamon
2.5 ml (½ tsp) ground ginger
60 g (2 oz) Brazil nuts, chopped
300 g (11 oz) carrot, grated
icing sugar or cream cheese icing

Beat oil, sugar and eggs well, add bicarbonate of soda and vanilla and beat again. Sift dry ingredients and beat into the mixture about one-third at a time. Add nuts and carrot, beat to combine. Pour into a sprayed or greased 25-cm (10-in) ring pan, microwave on 100% for 6-7 minutes. Allow to cool on a flat surface for 10 minutes before turning out onto a wire rack. Dust with sifted icing sugar or cover with cream cheese icing (page 92) before serving.

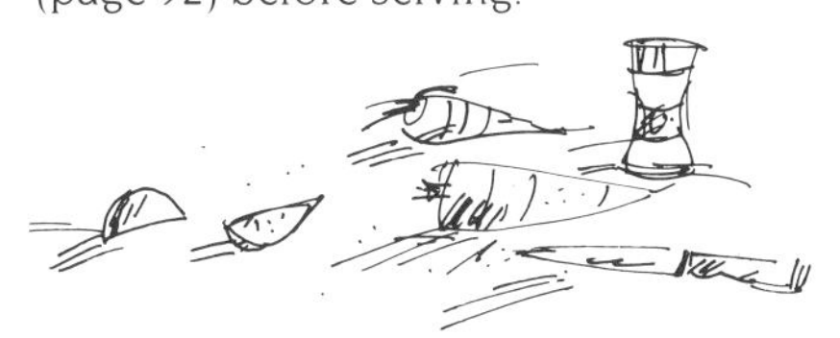

BUTTERMILK TEA RING

100%...3 minutes
plus Combination baking
Makes 1 ring cake

250 g (9 oz) butter
200 g (7 oz) sugar
3 eggs
30 ml (1 tbsp) chunky orange marmalade
300 g (11 oz) flour
pinch of salt
5 ml (1 tsp) baking powder
5 ml (1 tsp) bicarbonate of soda
200 ml (6½ fl oz) buttermilk
60 g (2 oz) desiccated coconut
125 g (4 oz) dates, chopped
200 g (7 oz) sultanas
generous pinch of salt

SYRUP
125 ml (4 fl oz) orange juice
90 g (3 oz) sugar
10 ml (2 tsp) orange liqueur

First make the syrup by microwaving all the ingredients in a jug on 100% for 3 minutes. Chill well.

Grease a heat-resistant ring pan. Cream butter and sugar very well until light and fluffy. Add eggs one at a time, beating well after each addition. Beat in the marmalade. Sift flour, salt and baking powder together. Dissolve the bicarbonate of soda in the buttermilk. Beat half the flour mixture and then half the liquid mixture into the creamed mixture. Add remaining flour and liquid, beating to combine. Stir in the coconut, dates, sultanas and salt. Turn into prepared pan. Bake according to instructions below. Allow cake to stand for 5 minutes, then pour the cold syrup over. Allow to stand for a further 15 minutes before turning out.

BROTHER
Hi-Speed at 220 °C for 18 minutes.

LEMON-GLAZED POUND CAKE

100%, 50%...28 minutes
Makes 1 large ring cake

60 g (2 oz) Marie biscuit crumbs
500 g (18 oz) sugar
300 g (11 oz) butter
5 eggs
few drops of vanilla essence
few drops of almond essence
2.5 ml (½ tsp) finely grated lemon rind
350 g (12 oz) plain flour
5 ml (1 tsp) baking powder
salt
250 ml (8 fl oz) evaporated milk

LEMON GLAZE
150 g (5 oz) sugar
185 ml (6 fl oz) sweet white wine
45 ml (3 tbsp) lemon juice
100 ml (3½ fl oz) orange juice
5 ml (1 tsp) grated lemon rind

Grease a large deep ring pan and sprinkle with biscuit crumbs to coat sides and base evenly. Beat sugar, butter, eggs, vanilla, almond essence and lemon rind to combine, then beat until light and fluffy. Sift flour, baking powder and salt and mix into sugar mixture alternately with milk. Turn batter into prepared pan and microwave on 50% for 15 minutes. Increase power to 100% and microwave for 5-8 minutes, or until top springs back when lightly touched. Stand for 10 minutes, then turn out onto a wire rack. With a skewer, make holes in the surface of the cake so the glaze can soak in.

To make the glaze, mix sugar, wine, lemon juice, orange juice and lemon rind together in a large glass bowl or jug. Microwave on 100% for 4-5 minutes, stirring at least once. Spoon glaze over the cake until absorbed. Cool, then sprinkle with icing sugar if desired.

Lemon-Glazed Pound Cake

HAWAIIAN CREAM TORTE

100%, 50%... 11 minutes
Makes 1 × 20-cm (8-in) layer cake

125 g (4 oz) plain flour
150 g (5 oz) sugar
7.5 ml (2½ tsp) baking powder
2.5 ml (½ tsp) salt
few drops of vanilla essence
2 eggs
75 ml (2½ fl oz) milk
75 g (2½ oz) butter, softened
250 ml (8 fl oz) whipping cream
30 g (1 oz) icing sugar
few drops of almond or rum essence
60 g (2 oz) crushed pineapple, well drained
45 g (1½ oz) desiccated coconut

Combine flour, sugar, baking powder, salt and vanilla in a mixing bowl. Add eggs, milk and butter. Beat on low speed of an electric mixer until well mixed, then beat at medium speed for 2 minutes, scraping bowl occasionally. Spread batter in a deep, greased and lined 20-cm (8-in) dish.

Microwave on 50% for 6 minutes, then on 100% for 2-5 minutes, or until done. Allow to stand for 5 minutes, then turn out and cool on a wire rack.

Slice cake in half horizontally to make two thin layers. Place bottom layer on a serving plate and set aside.

To complete the cake, whip cream with icing sugar and almond or rum essence to stiff peaks. Spread half the pineapple over the bottom cake layer. Top with a quarter of the cream mixture. Top with the remaining cake, spread remaining pineapple over the top and then spread remaining cream mixture over top and sides. Sprinkle with coconut and chill until ready to serve.

Hawaiian Cream Torte

EASTER SIMNEL CAKE

100%, 70%... 27 minutes
plus grill
Makes 1 × 23-cm (9-in) cake

200 g (7 oz) each currants and sultanas
150 g (5 oz) mixed peel
100 g (3½ oz) dates, chopped
150 g (5 oz) butter
200 g (7 oz) soft brown sugar
60 ml (4 tbsp) sherry
60 ml (4 tbsp) brandy
60 ml (4 tbsp) water
60 ml (4 tbsp) orange juice
45 g (1½ oz) glacé cherries, cut up
5 ml (1 tsp) bicarbonate of soda
5 ml (1 tsp) instant coffee granules
400 g (14 oz) marzipan
250 g (9 oz) plain flour
2.5 ml (½ tsp) baking powder
2.5 ml (½ tsp) ground ginger
generous pinch of ground nutmeg
3 eggs, lightly beaten
30 ml (2 tbsp) each brandy and sherry
1 egg white, lightly beaten

In a large bowl combine the currants, sultanas, mixed peel and dates. Add butter, sugar, sherry, brandy, water and orange juice. Cover with vented plastic wrap. Microwave on 100% for 5 minutes, stirring halfway through the cooking time. Stir in cherries, bicarbonate of soda and coffee, allow to cool. Roll out about 100 g (3½ oz) of the marzipan into a circle about 15-cm (6-in) in diameter, set aside. Sift flour, baking powder, ginger and nutmeg. Mix eggs into fruit mixture and then the sifted dry ingredients. Line the base of a deep round 23-cm (9-in) dish with parchment paper, grease or spray the sides. Spoon in a little more than half the mixture. Carefully place marzipan circle over the mixture. Spoon in remaining mixture. Cover with vented plastic wrap, microwave on 70% for 20-22 minutes. Stand until almost cool on a flat surface. Turn out onto a wire rack. Combine brandy and sherry, pour over cake. Roll out a second piece of marzipan large enough to cover the cake. Brush the top of the cake with egg white and place marzipan on top. Divide remaining marzipan into 11 balls, brush the base of each ball with egg white and place around the edge of the cake. Place under the grill for a few seconds to just brown. Decorate the sides of the cake with ribbon.

Greek Coconut Cake

GREEK COCONUT CAKE

100%...6 minutes
plus Combination baking
Makes 1 × 25-cm (10-in) ring cake

125 g (4 oz) desiccated coconut
125 ml (4 fl oz) milk
125 g (4 oz) butter
300 g (11 oz) sugar
6 eggs, separated
175 g (6 oz) plain flour
7.5 ml (1½ tsp) baking powder
75 ml (2½ fl oz) milk
SYRUP
400 g (14 oz) sugar
500 ml (16 fl oz) water
60 ml (4 tbsp) rum

Combine coconut and milk in a jug, microwave on 100% for 1 minute, then allow to stand for 15 minutes. Cream butter and half the sugar until light and fluffy, set aside. Beat egg yolks and remaining sugar until pale in colour. Combine the butter and yolk mixtures. Sift flour and baking powder, add alternately with the coconut and milk mixture. Beat in the extra milk. Beat whites to a soft peak consistency, fold into mixture. Spoon into a greased or sprayed 25-cm (10-in) ring pan. Bake according to the instructions below. Remove from oven and cool for 10 minutes before pouring syrup over the cake.

To make the syrup: combine sugar and water in a large jug, microwave on 100% for 5 minutes, stirring at least twice during that time. Stir in rum and cool slightly. Spoon syrup over cake, allow to cool completely before turning out. Serve plain or with cream.

BROTHER
Hi-Speed at 180 °C for 17-19 minutes.

Rigo Jansci

TURKISH CAKE

70%... 10 minutes
Makes 1 × 23-cm (9-in) ring cake

125 g (4 oz) butter
100 g (3½ oz) caster sugar
few drops of vanilla essence
3 eggs
45 g (1½ oz) cocoa powder
2.5 ml (½ tsp) cinnamon
pinch of ground cloves
generous pinch of ground nutmeg
125 ml (4 fl oz) milk
30 ml (2 tbsp) orange liqueur
175 g (6 oz) plain flour
7.5 ml (2½ tsp) baking powder
45 g (1½ oz) almonds, chopped
75 g (2½ oz) currants
75 g (2½ oz) mixed peel
30 g (1 oz) glacé cherries, chopped
1 ring glacé pineapple, chopped
TO DECORATE
2 rings glacé pineapple
glacé cherries
15 ml (1 tbsp) red currant or apple jelly

Cream butter and sugar until light and fluffy. Add vanilla and eggs one at a time, beating well after each addition. Beat in sifted cocoa powder and spices. In a jug combine milk and liqueur. Sift flour and baking powder. Add one-third of the flour to the creamed mixture, then one-third of the liquid. Add another third of the flour and remaining liquid. Combine the remaining flour with the nuts and fruit, mix into cake mixture. Turn into a well-greased 23-cm (9-in) ring pan and microwave on 70% for 7-9 minutes. Allow to cool on a flat surface before turning out. Decorate the top with pieces of fruit brushed with melted red currant jelly. To melt, microwave jelly on 70% for 30 seconds.

RIGO JANSCI

100%, 50%... 21 minutes
Makes 1 × 20-cm (8-in) cake

A quick and easy microwave version of the famous Hungarian speciality.

125 g (4 oz) plain flour
175 g (6 oz) caster sugar
15 g (½ oz) cocoa powder
10 ml (2 tsp) baking powder
3 eggs
125 ml (4 fl oz) warm water
125 ml (4 fl oz) oil
few drops of almond essence
5 ml (1 tsp) instant coffee granules
FILLING
250 ml (8 fl oz) whipping cream
200 g (7 oz) plain chocolate
45 ml (3 tbsp) dark rum
few drops of vanilla essence
GLAZE
150 g (5 oz) caster sugar
45 ml (3 tbsp) water
15 ml (1 tbsp) coffee liqueur
150 g (5 oz) plain chocolate

To make the cake, sift the flour, sugar, cocoa and baking powder together. Beat eggs, water, oil, essence and coffee powder together. Mix dry ingredients into the beaten mixture. Pour into a greased and lined round, deep 20-cm (8-in) dish. Microwave on 50% for 9 minutes and then on 100% for 1-2 minutes. Stand until cool on a flat surface before turning out onto a wire rack. When cold, split in half. Spread the filling very thickly onto the lower layer, place remaining layer on top. Pour warm glaze over the top of the cake. Refrigerate for at least 20 minutes before serving. Cut into very thin slices.

To make the filling, microwave cream and chocolate on 100% for 4-5 minutes, stirring every minute. Stir to combine well, then cool and refrigerate for 2 hours. Add rum and vanilla and beat until the mixture stands in soft peaks. Take care not to over beat.

To make the glaze, place all the ingredients into a jug, microwave on 100% for 4-5 minutes, stirring every minute. Mixture should actually boil. Cool for a few minutes before using. Should mixture thicken too much, microwave for a few seconds.

SOURED CREAM CINNAMON CAKE

100%... 10 minutes
Makes 1 × 25-cm (10-in) cake

100 g (3½ oz) sugar
60 g (2 oz) butter or margarine, softened
1 egg
few drops of vanilla essence
60 g (2 oz) wholemeal flour
60 g (2 oz) plain flour
2.5 ml (½ tsp) baking powder
2.5 ml (½ tsp) bicarbonate of soda
pinch of salt
185 ml (6 fl oz) soured cream

FILLING
45 g (1½ oz) soft brown sugar
30 g (1 oz) pecan nuts or hazelnuts, chopped
2.5 ml (½ tsp) cinnamon
pinch of ground nutmeg

GLAZE
30 g (1 oz) butter or margarine
125 g (4 oz) icing sugar, sifted
few drops of caramel essence
15-30 ml (1-2 tbsp) soured cream

For the cake, combine sugar, butter, egg and vanilla and beat on medium speed with an electric mixer for about 2 minutes. Then mix in sifted flours, baking powder, bicarbonate of soda and salt alternately with the soured cream.

To make the filling, combine all ingredients, mixing well. Spread half the batter in a 25-cm (10-in) round baking dish and sprinkle with half the filling. Repeat layers, then microwave on 100% for 5-7 minutes, or until the top springs back to the touch. Cool for 15 minutes before topping with the glaze.

To make the glaze, microwave butter in a deep jug on 100% for 2-3 minutes, or until lightly browned. Mix in icing sugar and caramel essence, then add soured cream, a little at a time until mixture is of desired consistency.

Serve warm, cut into wedges and topped with cream if desired.

Soured Cream Cinnamon Cake

CHOCOLATE SURPRISE CAKE

100%...8 minutes
Makes 1 × 23-cm (9-in) square cake

The delicious coconut filling is dropped by the spoonful into the chocolate batter before baking.

125 g (4 oz) plain flour
150 g (5 oz) sugar
30 g (1 oz) cocoa powder
2.5 ml (½ tsp) bicarbonate of soda
generous pinch of salt
few drops of vanilla essence
60 g (2 oz) butter or margarine
185 ml (6 fl oz) buttermilk
1 egg

FILLING
75 g (2½ oz) desiccated coconut
60 ml (4 tbsp) golden syrup
15 ml (1 tbsp) plain flour
few drops of almond essence
30 ml (2 tbsp) single cream

ICING
250 g (9 oz) icing sugar
15 g (½ oz) cocoa powder
45 g (1½ oz) butter, softened
few drops of vanilla essence
45 ml (3 tbsp) single cream
desiccated coconut, toasted

To make the cake, combine all ingredients and mix for about 3 minutes on medium speed of an electric mixer until smooth. Turn into a greased 23-cm (9-in) square baking dish and smooth the top.

To make the filling, combine all ingredients and mix well. Drop by the spoonful into the chocolate batter. Microwave on 100% for 5 minutes, check if nearly cooked, then microwave for 1½-2½ minutes more, or until a skewer inserted near the centre comes out clean. The top of the cake should still be moist. Cool completely before icing.

To make the icing, sift icing sugar and cocoa into a large bowl. Mix in butter and vanilla, then beat in the cream, a little at a time, until the mixture is of a spreading consistency. Spread over the cake, and sprinkle with toasted coconut. Cut into squares to serve.

Chocolate Surprise Cake

CARAMEL POUND CAKE WITH CHOCOLATE GLAZE

100%, 50%...16 minutes
Makes 1 large ring cake

1 packet vanilla cake mix
90 g (3 oz) packet caramel instant pudding mix
4 eggs
250 ml (8 fl oz) water
few drops of caramel essence
60 ml (4 tbsp) oil

GLAZE
90 g (3 oz) plain chocolate
30 g (1 oz) butter
300 g (11 oz) icing sugar, sifted
60 ml (4 tbsp) boiling water
pinch of salt

Combine cake mix, pudding mix, eggs, water, essence and oil. Blend on low speed of the electric mixer for 1 minute. Beat on medium speed for 3 minutes, then turn into a greased ring pan. Microwave on 100% for 8-12 minutes, or until a skewer inserted near the centre comes out clean. Stand for 10 minutes before turning out onto a wire rack and allowing to cool.

To make the glaze, microwave the chocolate on 50% for 2-3 minutes, or until melted. Stir in butter and microwave 1 minute more. Combine icing sugar, water, salt and chocolate mixture and beat until smooth. Spoon over the cooled cake.

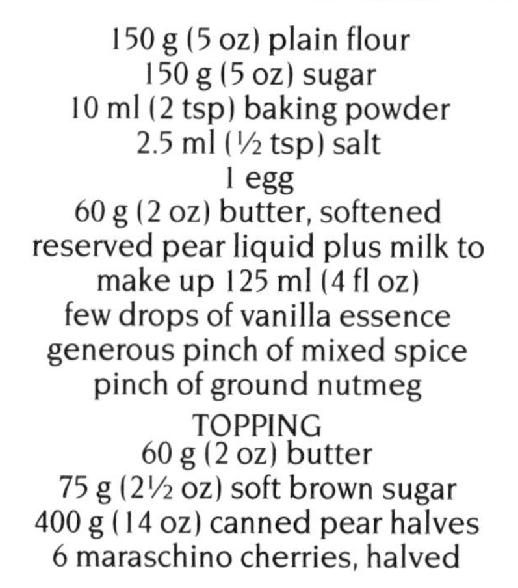

UPSIDE-DOWN PEAR CAKE

100%... 12 minutes
Makes 1 × 20-cm (8-in) cake

150 g (5 oz) plain flour
150 g (5 oz) sugar
10 ml (2 tsp) baking powder
2.5 ml (½ tsp) salt
1 egg
60 g (2 oz) butter, softened
reserved pear liquid plus milk to make up 125 ml (4 fl oz)
few drops of vanilla essence
generous pinch of mixed spice
pinch of ground nutmeg

TOPPING
60 g (2 oz) butter
75 g (2½ oz) soft brown sugar
400 g (14 oz) canned pear halves
6 maraschino cherries, halved

First make the topping: place butter in a 20-cm (8-in) round glass baking dish and microwave on 100% for 1 minute. Tilt dish to coat bottom evenly. Sprinkle brown sugar evenly over the bottom. Drain pears, reserving the liquid. Slice pears thickly. Arrange pear slices and cherries in the dish.

Place all ingredients for the cake in a bowl and beat on low speed for about 3 minutes until mixture is smooth. Spread mixture evenly over fruit. Place dish on inverted saucer and microwave on 100% for 9-11 minutes, or until a cocktail stick inserted near the centre comes out clean. Invert cake onto serving plate and let dish stand over cake for a few minutes. Serve warm or cool.

Upside-Down Pear Cake

ORANGE WINE CAKE

70%... 15 minutes
Makes 1 × 23-cm (9-in) square cake

1 orange
225 g (8 oz) plain flour
150 g (5 oz) raisins
5 ml (1 tsp) bicarbonate of soda
2.5 ml (½ tsp) salt
150 g (5 oz) sugar
125 g (4 oz) butter
2 eggs
250 ml (8 fl oz) buttermilk
few drops of vanilla essence
ICING
250 g (9 oz) icing sugar
reserved piece of orange rind
75 g (2½ oz) butter
1 egg white
about 45 ml (3 tbsp) dry sherry

Using a sharp knife, score the orange into 6 sections, remove the peel. Use the flesh for another purpose. Retain 1 piece of the orange rind for the icing. Fit a food processor bowl with the metal blade, process flour, raisins, bicarbonate of soda and salt until raisins are chopped, then set aside. Now process the sections of orange peel and half the sugar until finely chopped, add this to the flour mixture. Cream the remaining sugar with the butter until light in colour. Add eggs one at a time and mix well. Add buttermilk and vanilla and beat or process again. Add flour mixture and combine. Turn into a well-greased 23-cm (9-in) square dish. Microwave for 13-15 minutes on 70%. Allow to stand on a flat surface until cool. Spread with icing, then cut into squares and serve.

To make the icing, fit the work bowl of a food processor with the metal blade, process icing sugar and orange rind until rind is finely chopped. Add butter and process for about 20 seconds. Add the egg white and process again. Add the sherry a little at a time, until the icing is of a spreading consistency.

Orange Wine Cake

UPSIDE-DOWN GINGERBREAD

100%, 70%... 14 minutes
Makes 1 × 20-cm (8-in) square cake

100 g (3½ oz) butter or margarine
100 g (3½ oz) soft brown sugar
60 ml (4 tbsp) honey
2 eggs, beaten
225 g (8 oz) plain flour
15 ml (1 tbsp) ground ginger
5 ml (1 tsp) bicarbonate of soda
30 g (1 oz) mixed dried fruit or finely grated carrot
TOPPING
60 g (2 oz) butter or margarine
100 g (3½ oz) soft brown sugar
9 maraschino cherries, halved
400 g (14 oz) canned peach slices, drained

For the topping, place butter in a 20-cm (8-in) square baking dish and microwave on 100% for 1 minute. Sprinkle with brown sugar. Arrange peach slices in rows. Add cherries at intervals.

For the cake, place butter, sugar and honey in a bowl and microwave for 3 minutes. Cool slightly, then beat in the eggs. Sift dry ingredients together and fold into the egg mixture with dried fruit or grated carrot. Carefully spoon mixture over peaches. Smooth top and shield corners with aluminium foil. Microwave on 70% for 9-10 minutes. The gingerbread should begin to pull away from the sides of the pan and feel almost dry to the touch.

Allow to stand for 5 minutes, then invert onto a serving dish. Leave the baking dish over the cake for another 5 minutes. Serve with cream or custard.

DESSERTS

Coffee Crème Caramel; Chocolate Fudge Cheesecake Wedges; Apricot & Almond Crumble

MOST people love desserts and puddings and with the help of a microwave oven popular desserts such as crème caramel, hot fruit puddings, Christmas puddings and cheesecakes can be made quickly and with little fuss. Some of the puddings in this chapter use similar techniques to those of cakes and pies, so please read those chapters for help with baked puddings. Many puddings and desserts benefit from the use of a combination microwave oven, so we have included some delicious recipes for you to try.

COFFEE CRÈME CARAMEL

100%, 50%, 30%... 23 minutes
Serves 6-8

4 eggs
60 g (2 oz) caster sugar
few drops of vanilla essence
60 ml (4 tbsp) coffee liqueur
500 ml (16 fl oz) milk

CARAMEL
45 g (1½ oz) sugar
35 ml (7 tsp) water
45 ml (3 tbsp) coffee liqueur

Blend eggs, caster sugar, vanilla and coffee liqueur with milk in a liquidizer. Strain into a jug.

For the caramel, place sugar and water in a glass ring dish and microwave on 100% for 3 minutes. Check for colour, then microwave 2-3 minutes more, or until golden brown. Tip caramel around the base and sides of the dish. Pour egg mixture over caramel and cover with vented plastic wrap. Microwave on 100% for 2 minutes, on 50% for 3 minutes and then on 30% for 8-12 minutes or until beginning to set. Remove plastic and cool, then chill well. Turn out onto a plate and pour coffee liqueur over. Serve with cream.

CHERRY BROWNIE PUDDING

70%... 19 minutes
Serves 8

60 g (2 oz) plain chocolate
60 g (2 oz) butter or margarine
200 g (7 oz) sugar
few drops of vanilla essence
2 eggs
400 g (14 oz) canned cherry pie filling
125 g (4 oz) plain flour
2.5 ml (½ tsp) baking powder
2.5 ml (½ tsp) salt
60 ml (4 tbsp) water
30 g (1 oz) butter or margarine

Microwave chocolate on 70% for 2 minutes, stir to melt. Add butter and stir until melted. Beat in the sugar, vanilla and eggs. Add 225 g (8 oz) of the pie filling, the flour, baking powder and salt. Mix well. Combine remaining pie filling, water and 30 g (1 oz) butter in a 20-cm (8-in) square baking dish. Microwave for 1-2 minutes to melt butter. Stir, then spoon chocolate mixture over cherries and microwave on 70% for 12-15 minutes, or until top springs back when touched. The top should still look moist. Stand for 10 minutes then serve warm with cream or ice cream.

CHOCOLATE FUDGE CHEESECAKE WEDGES

70%... 4 minutes
plus Combination baking
Serves 8-10

It's easy to mix and quick to bake with a convection/microwave oven.

1 recipe basic crumb crust mixture (page 86)
250 g (9 oz) cream cheese, softened
125 ml (4 fl oz) mayonnaise
30 ml (2 tbsp) single cream
100 g (3½ oz) sugar
2 extra large eggs
200 g (7 oz) plain chocolate
few drops of vanilla essence

Press the crumb crust mixture onto the base and sides of a 5-cm (2-in) deep, 20-cm (8-in) round baking dish and set aside. Combine cream cheese, mayonnaise and cream and beat until smooth. Mix in sugar, then beat in eggs one at a time. Place chocolate in a large bowl and microwave on 70% for 3-4 minutes, or until melted. Stir into the cheese mixture along with the vanilla. Pour into the prepared crust and bake according to instructions below. Cool on a wire rack, then chill. Serve with cream or soured cream if desired.

BROTHER
Hi-Speed at 250 °C for 14-16 minutes.

APRICOT & ALMOND CRUMBLE

100%... 6 minutes
Serves 6

250 g (9 oz) dried apricots, quartered
1 small piece cinnamon stick
strip of lemon rind
250 ml (8 fl oz) water
30 ml (2 tbsp) orange liqueur
about 60 g (2 oz) sugar
60 g (2 oz) stale cake crumbs

TOPPING
75 g (2½ oz) soft brown sugar
30 g (1 oz) rolled oats
45 g (1½ oz) plain flour
30 g (1 oz) ground almonds
75 g (2½ oz) butter

TO SERVE
250 ml (8 fl oz) soured cream

Place apricots, cinnamon stick, lemon rind, water, orange liqueur and sugar in a bowl. Cover with vented plastic wrap, microwave on 100% for 2 minutes. Allow to stand for 10 minutes, then remove piece of cinnamon stick and lemon rind. Divide cake crumbs between 6 ramekins, and spoon some of the apricot mixture into each ramekin.

To make the topping, combine sugar, oats, flour and ground almonds, rub in the butter. Sprinkle over the top of the apricots. Arrange ramekins in a circle in the microwave, cook on 100% for 4 minutes. Serve warm with soured cream.

SPICY STEAMED PUDDING

100%, 70%... 19 minutes
Serves 10

220 ml (7 fl oz) water
30 ml (2 tbsp) brandy
150 g (5 oz) sultanas
30 g (1 oz) butter
100 g (3½ oz) sugar
150 g (5 oz) molasses
1 egg
175 g (6 oz) plain flour
5 ml (1 tsp) bicarbonate of soda
5 ml (1 tsp) salt
2.5 ml (½ tsp) cinnamon
pinch of ground nutmeg

Microwave water on 100% for 3 minutes, add brandy and pour over sultanas and stand until cool. Beat butter with sugar, molasses and egg. Sift dry ingredients together and add to butter mixture along with the sultanas and water. Mix well and pour into a greased 2-litre (3½-pint) ring. Cover with vented plastic wrap and microwave on 70% for 14-16 minutes, or until pudding appears set but still glossy. Remove from the microwave, allow to stand for 15 minutes, then turn out onto a wire rack to cool. When cool, wrap well and keep in the refrigerator for a couple of days to mature before serving. Reheat on 50% for 4-6 minutes and serve with custard.

APPLE RAISIN MERINGUE

100%, 70%... 14 minutes
Serves 4

1 kg (2¼ lb) Granny Smith apples
15 ml (1 tbsp) water
60 g (2 oz) seedless raisins
2 egg yolks
brown sugar to taste
2.5 ml (½ tsp) cinnamon
30 ml (2 tbsp) brandy

TOPPING
2 egg whites
90 g (3 oz) caster sugar

Peel, core and slice apples. Place in a bowl with water. Cover with vented plastic wrap and microwave on 100% for 4-5 minutes. Cool, then purée. Add raisins, egg yolks, sugar, cinnamon and brandy. Spoon mixture into a deep 20-cm (8-in) round dish.

For the topping, beat egg whites until stiff, then beat in half the sugar a little at a time. Carefully fold in the remaining sugar and spoon the mixture over the apples. Microwave on 70% for 7-9 minutes until the meringue is set.

BROWN SUGAR CHEESECAKE CUPS

50%, 30%, 15%... 11 minutes
Serves 6

6 Marie biscuits, crushed
250 g (9 oz) cream cheese
75 g (2½ oz) soft brown sugar
2 large eggs
few drops of vanilla essence
10 ml (2 tsp) grated lemon rind
10 ml (2 tsp) lemon juice
30 g (1 oz) soft brown sugar

Divide crushed biscuits between 6 ramekins and set aside. Soften cream cheese if necessary by microwaving on 15% for 1 minute. Add brown sugar, eggs and vanilla. Beat until smooth. Stir in lemon rind and lemon juice. Divide mixture among the ramekins. Arrange ramekins in a circle in the microwave and microwave on 30% for 7 minutes, then on 50% for 2-3 minutes. Remove from the oven and sprinkle brown sugar over each ramekin. Cool for 1 hour, then chill well.

Serve topped with whipped cream or soured cream and fruit such as grapes, kiwi fruit or strawberries.

BANANA-FILLED CRÊPES

100%... 8 minutes
Serves 6

12 crêpes (page 93)
90 g (3 oz) butter
60 g (2 oz) soft brown sugar
grated rind and juice of 1 lemon
5 ml (1 tsp) cinnamon
6 ripe bananas, sliced
75 ml (2½ fl oz) dark rum

TO SERVE
ground nutmeg
250 ml (8 fl oz) whipping cream, whipped

Place butter in a browning dish, microwave on 100% for 2 minutes, add brown sugar, microwave for 1 minute more. Stir in lemon juice, rind and cinnamon. Microwave for 3 minutes, stirring twice during the cooking time. Add bananas, toss to coat with the mixture, microwave for 1 minute. Heat rum in a measuring jug for 1 minute. Pour over the bananas and ignite. Divide the mixture between the crêpes and fold into quarters. Dust with nutmeg and serve with whipped cream.

AMARETTO CHEESECAKE

100%, 70%... 11 minutes
Makes 1 × 23-cm (9-in) pie

CRUST
100 g (3½ oz) digestive biscuits, crushed
generous pinch of cinnamon
60 g (2 oz) butter
30 ml (2 tbsp) Amaretto

FILLING
60 g (2 oz) marzipan
75 g (2½ oz) sugar
20 ml (4 tsp) plain flour
500 g (18 oz) cream cheese
60 ml (4 tbsp) Amaretto
3 eggs
170 ml (5½ fl oz) soured cream
2.5 ml (½ tsp) finely grated lemon rind

TO DECORATE
90 ml (3 fl oz) whipping cream, whipped
toasted flaked almonds

First make the crust: combine biscuit crumbs and cinnamon in a bowl. Microwave butter on 100% for 1 minute, stir into crumbs together with Amaretto and mix to combine. Turn crumb mixture into a greased 23-cm (9-in) pie plate. Using the back of a spoon, press to form a crust. Chill for 10 minutes.

To make the filling, crumble marzipan into a bowl, add sugar, flour, cream cheese and liqueur, beat well. Beat in eggs one at a time, then beat in the soured cream and lemon rind. Microwave the mixture on 70% for 8-10 minutes, whisking the mixture well every 2 minutes. Pour into the chilled shell and refrigerate for 3 hours. Decorate top with whipped cream and toasted almonds.

Amaretto Cheesecake

OEUFS À LA NEIGE

100%, 50%... 11 minutes
Serves 6

250 ml (8 fl oz) milk
1 vanilla pod
3 eggs, separated
pinch of salt
75 g (2½ oz) caster sugar
100 ml (3½ fl oz) single cream
30 ml (2 tbsp) Amaretto
1 recipe caramel syrup (page 93)
30 g (1 oz) toasted flaked almonds (see *NOTE*)

Microwave milk and vanilla in a shallow casserole on 100% for 3 minutes. Allow to stand for 5 minutes, then remove vanilla pod. Beat egg whites and salt until stiff, then gradually beat in half the sugar. Drop 4 or 5 spoonfuls of the mixture into the milk, microwave for about 1 minute until set. Using a slotted spoon, lift off the puffs and drain on paper towel. Repeat until all the egg white mixture has been used up, about 4 batches in all. Strain the milk. Whisk yolks and remaining sugar until thick and pale, add milk, cream and Amaretto and beat to combine. Pour into a jug, microwave on 50% for 3-4 minutes, whisking every 30 seconds. Place a piece of greaseproof paper directly on top of the custard to prevent a skin from forming, then chill. Pour into a shallow serving dish, float 'islands' on top of custard, drizzle liberally with caramel and sprinkle with nuts. Serve as soon as possible.

NOTE To toast the almonds, place slivered nuts in a browning dish and microwave on 100% for 4-5 minutes, stirring every minute.

Oeufs à la Neige

CREAM CHEESE BLINTZES

70%... 5 minutes
Makes 12-14

500 g (18 oz) cream cheese
few drops of vanilla essence
1 egg
30 g (1 oz) caster sugar
10 ml (2 tsp) custard powder
12-14 thick crêpes (page 93)
30 g (1 oz) caster sugar
5 ml (1 tsp) cinnamon

Beat cream cheese, vanilla, egg, caster sugar and custard powder together. Spoon about 45 ml (3 tbsp) of the filling on one side of each pancake. Fold in the sides, then roll up. Place each blintz seam-side down in a shallow dish.

Cover with vented plastic wrap, microwave on 70% for 4-5 minutes, until piping hot.

Combine cinnamon and sugar, sprinkle over the blintzes and serve immediately.

PINEAPPLE RICE PUDDING WITH MERINGUE

100%, 70%, 50%... 53 minutes
plus Grill
Serves 6

75 g (2½ oz) rice
45 g (1½ oz) caster sugar
600 ml (19 fl oz) milk
15 g (½ oz) butter
200 ml (6½ fl oz) single cream
400 g (14 oz) canned pineapple chunks, drained
10 ml (2 tsp) chopped preserved ginger
3 eggs, separated
100 g (3½ oz) caster sugar

Place rice, sugar, milk and butter in a large bowl, microwave on 100% for 8 minutes, stirring twice. Add cream, reduce power to 50%, microwave for 25-30 minutes, stirring every 5 minutes. Cover and allow to stand for 10 minutes. Stir in pineapple chunks, ginger and egg yolks. Pour into a greased 20-cm (8-in) pie plate, cover and microwave for 5 minutes. Beat egg whites until stiff, gradually beat in caster sugar until stiff peaks form. Spread on top of the rice mixture. Microwave on 70% for 9-10 minutes until set. Place under the grill for a few minutes to brown the edges. Serve hot.

SUMMER PUDDING

70%...7 minutes
Serves 6

Use fruits such as fresh strawberries or frozen raspberries for this classic summer dessert.

CAKE
2 eggs
60 g (2 oz) caster sugar
few drops of vanilla essence
few drops of almond essence
60 g (2 oz) plain flour
generous pinch of baking powder
5 ml (1 tsp) grated lemon rind

FRUIT MIXTURE
650 g (1½ lb) soft red fruit such as strawberries, raspberries, redcurrants or loganberries
60 g (2 oz) caster sugar
30 ml (2 tbsp) fruit liqueur

To make the cake, beat eggs and sugar with vanilla and almond essence until very light. Sift flour with the baking powder, stir in the lemon rind and fold into the egg mixture. Gently turn into a deep, greased and lined 18-cm (7-in) cake pan and microwave on 70% for 3-4 minutes, or until just firm. Stand until cool, then turn out and slice horizontally to form 3 layers.

Using 2 layers, cut pieces to fit the bottom and sides of a pudding basin. Combine fruits, sugar and liqueur. Cover and microwave on 70% for 3 minutes. Using a slotted spoon, spoon mixture into the prepared basin. Cover with the third slice of cake to form a lid. Pour juices over the pudding. Cover with plastic wrap, then weight the top and refrigerate overnight. Turn out, cut into wedges and serve with cream.

Summer Pudding

HONEYED PEAR CAKE

100%...7 minutes
plus Combination baking
Serves 6-8

60 ml (4 tbsp) honey
30 g (1 oz) butter
generous pinch of cinnamon
pinch of ground cloves
5 ml (1 tsp) grated lemon rind
15 ml (1 tbsp) lemon juice
15 ml (1 tbsp) brandy
4 large pears, peeled, cored and sliced

TOPPING
100 g (3½ oz) butter
75 g (2½ oz) caster sugar
2 eggs
100 g (3½ oz) ground almonds
few drops of vanilla essence
15 g (½ oz) plain flour

Place honey and butter into a 23-cm (9-in) pie plate, microwave on 100% for 2 minutes. Stir well and add spices, lemon rind and juice. Microwave for a further 2 minutes. Stir in brandy and pears, microwave for 3 minutes.

Meanwhile make the topping. Cream butter and sugar very well, add eggs one at a time, beating well after each addition. Carefully fold in the ground almonds, vanilla essence and flour. Spread over the pears. Bake according to instructions below. Serve warm with cream or custard.

BROTHER
Hi-Speed at 160 °C for 10 minutes, then on Convection for 3-4 minutes.

CHOCOLATE SHERRY SOUFFLÉS

50%...5 minutes
plus Combination baking
Serves 6

Use the convection microwave to bake these delicious desserts

4 eggs, separated
75 g (2½ oz) caster sugar
15 g (½ oz) plain flour
2 ripe bananas, mashed
few drops of vanilla essence
30 ml (2 tbsp) medium cream sherry
100 g (3½ oz) plain chocolate, broken up

Combine egg yolks, sugar, flour, bananas, vanilla and sherry in a mixing bowl and beat for 3 minutes until light. Microwave chocolate for 4-5 minutes on 50% stirring occasionally until melted.

Honeyed Pear Cake

Add to the egg mixture and stir to combine thoroughly. Beat egg whites to soft peaks and fold into the chocolate mixture. Divide the mixture between 6 greased soufflé dishes (250 ml (8 fl oz) capacity) and bake according to instructions below. Serve immediately.

BROTHER
Hi-Speed at 180 °C for 13-15 minutes.

BAKED HAWAIIAN PINEAPPLE

100%...8 minutes
Serves 6

1 large ripe pineapple
60 g (2 oz) seedless green grapes
45 ml (3 tbsp) light rum
45 g (1½ oz) soft brown sugar
30 ml (2 tbsp) desiccated coconut

SAUCE
75 g (2½ oz) sugar
15 g (½ oz) cornflour
125 ml (4 fl oz) single cream
250 ml (8 fl oz) coconut cream (page 92)
few drops of vanilla essence

First make the sauce: mix sugar and cornflour, stir in cream and coconut cream.

Microwave for 2 minutes on 100%, stir well, then microwave for 2 minutes more, or until slightly thickened. Stir in vanilla and chill. Cut the pineapple in half lengthways, leaving crown on. Remove fruit from pineapple halves, leaving a shell. Cube fruit, add grapes, rum and brown sugar. Place fruit in pineapple shells, cover with vented plastic wrap and microwave on 100% for 2-4 minutes, depending on the size of the pineapple. Top with the coconut sauce and sprinkle with desiccated coconut.

Baked Hawaiian Pineapple

Orange & Cream Cheese Squares

ORANGE & CREAM CHEESE SQUARES

100%, 50%... 14 minutes
Serves 8

175 g (6 oz) plain flour
200 g (7 oz) sugar
60 g (2 oz) pecan nuts, chopped
2.5 ml (½ tsp) cinnamon
generous pinch of ground ginger
75 g (2½ oz) margarine
125 ml (4 fl oz) boiling water
30 ml (2 tbsp) treacle
30 ml (2 tbsp) golden syrup
100 g (3½ oz) dates, chopped
7.5 ml (1½ tsp) bicarbonate of soda

TOPPING
75 g (2½ oz) low-fat soft cheese
45 g (1½ oz) caster sugar
few drops of vanilla essence
100 ml (3½ fl oz) whipping cream

SAUCE
75 ml (2½ fl oz) frozen orange juice
150 ml (5 fl oz) water
30 g (1 oz) margarine
2.5 ml (½ tsp) grated orange rind
15 ml (1 tbsp) lemon juice
15 g (½ oz) cornflour
about 30 g (1 oz) sugar

Place flour, sugar, nuts and spices in a bowl, add margarine and rub in. Spoon half the crumble over the base of a greased 25 × 15-cm (10 × 6-in) dish. Press down firmly. Combine the remaining ingredients and stand for a few minutes. Spoon over base and sprinkle with remaining crumble. Shield the corners of the dish with foil. Stand dish on a saucer, microwave on 50% for 6 minutes, then on 100% for 4-6 minutes. Stand for 10 minutes before cutting into squares. Serve topped with cream cheese topping and orange sauce.

To make the topping, beat cream cheese, sugar and vanilla well. Then add cream and beat until peaking consistency. Chill until required.

To make the sauce, mix all the ingredients in a large jug, microwave on 100% for 1½-2 minutes, beating every 30 seconds. Serve hot.

HAZELNUT & POPPY GATEAU

100%, 70%... 7 minutes
Serves 10-12

60 ml (4 tbsp) poppy seeds
45 g (1½ oz) hazelnuts, toasted
45 ml (3 tbsp) self-raising flour
75 g (2½ oz) soft brown sugar
4 eggs, separated
few drops of vanilla essence

FILLING
200 ml (6½ fl oz) whipping cream
30 g (1 oz) sugar
15-30 ml (1-2 tbsp) brandy

GLAZE
100 g (3½ oz) plain chocolate
15 g (½ oz) butter
45 ml (3 tbsp) single cream
toasted hazelnuts to decorate

Lightly grease a 20-cm (8-in) microwave ring pan, then line the bottom with waxed paper. Set aside.

Grind poppy seeds in a spice mill, food processor or mortar and pestle. Place hazelnuts in a food processor and process until finely ground. Add poppy seeds and flour and blend well. Add 30 ml (2 tbsp) of the sugar to the egg yolks and beat until light. Mix in vanilla essence. Fold in flour mixture. Beat egg whites to soft peaks and gradually beat in remaining sugar. Fold the egg white mixture into the yolks. Turn into prepared pan and microwave on 100% for 3-3½ minutes. Allow to stand for 8 minutes, then turn out onto a wire rack to cool. Cut the gateau in half horizontally.

To make the filling, beat cream to stiff peaks and fold in sugar and brandy. Spread over the bottom layer of the gateau and replace the top.

To make the glaze, microwave chocolate on 70% for 3 minutes, stirring every minute. Mix in butter and cream. Use to ice the gateau, then decorate with hazelnuts and chill until ready to serve.

NOTE For an extra special filling fold 100 g (3½ oz) sliced strawberries into the cream.

Rum Nut Tartlets

100%...7 minutes
Makes 12

60 g (2 oz) butter
100 g (3½ oz) Marie biscuit crumbs
30 g (1 oz) soft brown sugar

FILLING
75 g (2½ oz) pecan nuts, coarsely chopped
3 eggs
150 g (5 oz) golden syrup
75 g (2½ oz) soft brown sugar
30 g (1 oz) butter
15 ml (1 tbsp) plain flour
few drops of vanilla essence
few drops of rum essence or 10 ml (2 tsp) dark rum

Place two paper baking cups in each cup of a microwave muffin pan. Microwave 60 g (2 oz) butter on 100% for 45 seconds. Stir into crumbs together with brown sugar. Divide half the mixture among the paper cups. Reserve remaining mixture.

For the filling, divide half the nuts among the cups. Reserve remaining nuts. Mix eggs, golden syrup, brown sugar, butter, flour, vanilla and rum. Spoon half the mixture into prepared cups and microwave on 100% for 2-3 minutes or until quite firm on top. Repeat assembly and baking with remaining crumbs, nuts and filling mixture.

Christmas Pudding

50%...25 minutes
Serves 8

75 g (2½ oz) sultanas
100 g (3½ oz) raisins
75 g (2½ oz) currants
60 g (2 oz) mixed peel
60 g (2 oz) cherries, cut up
45 g (1½ oz) cashew nuts, chopped
1 small carrot, grated
60 g (2 oz) moist brown sugar
15 ml (1 tbsp) molasses
1 apple, grated
45 ml (3 tbsp) brandy
75 ml (2½ fl oz) beer
grated rind and juice of half a lemon
3 eggs, beaten
60 g (2 oz) plain flour
75 g (2½ oz) suet, finely shredded
60 g (2 oz) fresh white breadcrumbs
10 ml (2 tsp) gravy browning
2.5 ml (½ tsp) mixed spice
generous pinch of ground nutmeg
few drops of almond essence

Combine in a large bowl dried fruit, nuts, carrot, brown sugar, molasses, apple, brandy, beer, lemon rind and juice. Stand for 1 hour. Add the remaining ingredients and mix very well. Grease or spray a 1-litre (1¾-pint) pudding basin. Place mixture in pudding basin, cover with vented plastic wrap. Microwave on 50% for 20-25 minutes. Stand until cool. Sprinkle with a little extra brandy and cover tightly with aluminium foil. Store until required.

Pumpkin Pudding

100%, 70%...16 minutes
Makes 1 × 25-cm (10-in) ring

250 g (9 oz) plain flour
2.5 ml (½ tsp) salt
7.5 ml (1½ tsp) cinnamon
5 ml (1 tsp) ground allspice
7.5 ml (1½ tsp) bicarbonate of soda
2.5 ml (½ tsp) baking powder
3 eggs
150 g (5 oz) soft brown sugar
60 ml (4 tbsp) treacle
125 ml (4 fl oz) oil
350 g (12 oz) cooked, mashed pumpkin
125 ml (4 fl oz) buttermilk
60 g (2 oz) macadamia nuts, finely chopped

Sift the dry ingredients together. Beat eggs, brown sugar and treacle together in a bowl until thick, then beat in the oil, beating well. Stir in pumpkin and flour mixture alternately with buttermilk. Lastly stir in the nuts. Turn mixture into a greased 25-cm (10-in) ring pan. Cover with vented plastic wrap. Microwave on 70% for 10-12 minutes, then on 100% for 3-4 minutes. Stand for 5 minutes before turning out and serving with custard.

Banana & Sultana Dumplings In Rum Sauce

100%...12 minutes
Serves 6

These delicious dumplings are cooked in a rum sauce. Serve with cream.

DUMPLINGS
45 g (1½ oz) plain flour
30 g (1 oz) wholemeal flour
5 ml (1 tsp) baking powder
2.5 ml (½ tsp) salt
30 g (1 oz) butter or margarine
45 g (1½ oz) brown sugar
60 g (2 oz) sultanas
2 ripe bananas
75 ml (2½ fl oz) milk
few drops of vanilla essence
few drops of caramel essence

SAUCE
30 g (1 oz) butter or margarine
300 g (11 oz) soft brown sugar
375 ml (12 fl oz) water
few drops of vanilla essence
30 ml (2 tbsp) rum

First make the sauce: combine butter, sugar, water and vanilla in a large jug and microwave on 100% for 5-6 minutes, stirring twice. Stir in the rum.

For the dumplings, combine flours, baking powder and salt. Rub in butter and stir in sugar and sultanas. Mash the bananas and combine with the remaining ingredients. Add to flour mixture, stirring until just combined.

Transfer hot sauce to a deep, 20-cm (8-in) baking dish and drop banana mixture by the spoonful into the sauce. Cover and microwave on 100% for 5-6 minutes. Stand, covered for 5 minutes before serving.

GALLIANO PUDDING

100%... 14 minutes
Serves 6-8

A great pudding to serve on a cool evening.

30 g (1 oz) butter or margarine
100 g (3½ oz) sugar
45 g (1½ oz) soft brown sugar
1 egg
125 g (4 oz) plain flour
5 ml (1 tsp) baking powder
2.5 ml (½ tsp) salt
15 ml (1 tbsp) grated orange rind
150 ml (5 fl oz) water

SAUCE
250 ml (8 fl oz) water
125 ml (4 fl oz) orange juice
100 g (3½ oz) caster sugar
45 g (1½ oz) soft brown sugar
60 g (2 oz) butter
5 ml (1 tsp) grated lemon rind
45 ml (3 tbsp) Galliano

Microwave butter on 100% for 30 seconds. Add sugars and egg, mix well. Combine flour, baking powder, salt and orange rind, add to butter mixture. Beat until smooth, then gradually stir in water. Turn into an ungreased 20-cm (8-in) baking dish. The batter will be thin.

For the sauce, combine water and orange juice. Microwave for about 4 minutes or until boiling. Add sugars and butter. Stir to melt. Add lemon rind and Galliano, mixing well. Carefully pour the sauce over the cake batter and microwave on 100% for 7-9 minutes or until a skewer inserted near the centre comes out clean. Serve warm.

QUICK APPLE & GOOSEBERRY PUDDING

Combination baking
Serves 6-8

400 g (14 oz) canned apple pie filling
400 g (14 oz) canned gooseberries

TOPPING
75 g (2½ oz) plain flour
1 egg
45 g (1½ oz) sugar
5 ml (1 tsp) baking powder
pinch of salt
60 g (2 oz) very soft margarine
60 ml (4 tbsp) milk

Spoon apples into a 20-cm (8-in) shallow casserole. Drain gooseberries, reserving the juice. Add gooseberries and about 60 ml (4 tbsp) of the juice to the apples. Place all ingredients for the topping in a bowl. Beat very well with an electric mixer for about 2 minutes. Spread on top of the fruit. Bake as per chart below. Serve warm with cream or custard.

BROTHER
Hi-Speed at 200 °C for 13-15 minutes.

LAYERED FRUIT CHRISTMAS PUDDING

100%, 50%... 22 minutes
Serves 8-10

CAKE
175 g (6 oz) butter or margarine
175 g (6 oz) soft brown sugar
2 eggs
15 ml (1 tbsp) golden syrup
30 ml (2 tbsp) orange juice
few drops of rum essence or
10 ml (2 tsp) dark rum
250 g (9 oz) plain flour
15 ml (1 tbsp) baking powder
2.5 ml (½ tsp) salt
30 ml (2 tbsp) grated orange rind

FRUIT FILLING
60 g (2 oz) butter or margarine
60 g (2 oz) soft brown sugar
2 apples, peeled, cored and grated
100 g (3½ oz) raisins or sultanas
30 ml (2 tbsp) chopped glacé cherries
45 g (1½ oz) pecan nuts or hazelnuts, chopped
45 ml (3 tbsp) chopped mixed peel
4 eggs, separated
5 ml (1 tsp) mixed spice
5 ml (1 tsp) cinnamon
2.5 ml (½ tsp) ground nutmeg
generous pinch of ground cloves
generous pinch of ground allspice

To make the sponge, cream butter and sugar until light. Combine eggs, golden syrup, orange juice and rum and beat into the creamed mixture. Combine flour, baking powder, salt and orange rind and fold into the creamed mixture.

To make the filling, combine butter and sugar and microwave on 100% for 2 minutes. Stir to dissolve sugar. Add remaining ingredients, mix well.

To assemble, grease a deep pudding basin or glass bowl and line with plastic wrap. Grease the plastic wrap. Spread a little of the cake mixture in the bottom of the bowl, then top with a little of the fruit mixture, spreading evenly. Repeat layers, ending with sponge, making 4 layers of the cake mixture and 3 layers of the fruit filling.

Cover loosely with plastic wrap and microwave on 100% for 12-15 minutes. If the top is done before the bottom, cover with foil, then microwave for 1 minute more. Cool for about 20 minutes in the bowl before turning out onto a serving plate. Reheat when required on 50% for 3-4 minutes. To serve cut in wedges and top with rum and orange sauce (page 92).

DATE DESSERT

70%, 50%... 12 minutes
Serves 6-8

90 g (3 oz) plain flour
2.5 ml (½ tsp) bicarbonate of soda
salt
100 g (3½ oz) soft brown sugar
60 g (2 oz) margarine, softened
2 eggs
few drops of vanilla essence
125 ml (4 fl oz) soured cream
125 g (4 oz) dates, chopped
30 g (1 oz) pecan nuts, chopped

TOPPING
125 ml (4 fl oz) soured cream
45 ml (3 tbsp) single cream
45 g (1½ oz) soft brown sugar

Sift flour, bicarbonate of soda and salt into a bowl. Add brown sugar, margarine, eggs, vanilla essence and soured cream. Mix well, then stir in dates and pecans.

Pour into a greased deep 25-cm (10-in) pie plate. Place pie plate on top of an inverted saucer. Microwave on 50% for 6 minutes, and then on 70% for a further 5 minutes. Remove from microwave and allow to cool for 10 minutes before pouring cream topping over.

To make the topping: combine all ingredients in a bowl, then microwave on 50% for 30 seconds.

Serve dessert warm. To reheat, cover and microwave on 50% for 2-3 minutes, depending on the size of the piece being reheated.

Layered Fruit Christmas Pudding

ALMOND FRUIT CRUNCH

100%... 19 minutes
Serves 9-12

400 g (14 oz) canned cherry pie filling
150 g (5 oz) crushed pineapple
30 g (1 oz) sugar
few drops of almond essence
75 g (2½ oz) butter
60 g (2 oz) plain flour
90 g (3 oz) rolled oats
30 g (1 oz) All-Bran cereal
100 g (3½ oz) soft brown sugar
2.5 ml (½ tsp) cinnamon
45 g (1½ oz) flaked almonds, toasted

Combine pie filling, pineapple, sugar and almond essence. Microwave butter on 100% for 1 minute, add cake flour, oats, All-Bran, brown sugar and cinnamon. Coarsely chop the almonds and stir into the flour mixture. Press half the mixture onto the base of a 20-cm (8-in) baking dish and spread fruit mixture on top. Sprinkle with remaining crumb mixture and microwave for 14-18 minutes, until heated through and bubbly. Cut in squares and serve topped with ice cream or cream.

Citrus & Ginger Cheesecake

CITRUS & GINGER CHEESECAKE

100%... 1 minute
plus Combination baking
Serves 8-10

CRUST
10 Marie biscuits
6 ginger nut biscuits
30 g (1 oz) soft brown sugar
2.5 ml (½ tsp) cinnamon
60 g (2 oz) butter
30 ml (2 tbsp) single cream

FILLING
250 g (9 oz) cream cheese, softened
125 ml (4 fl oz) mayonnaise
100 g (3½ oz) caster sugar
3 large eggs
15 ml (1 tbsp) grated orange rind
15 ml (1 tbsp) lemon juice
few drops of vanilla essence
whipped cream and lemon or orange slices to decorate

To make the crust, break up biscuits and place in a food processor or blender. Process to fine crumbs. Add brown sugar and cinnamon, pulsing to mix in. Microwave butter for 30-45 seconds on 100%, then add to the crumbs and mix in. Stir in the cream and press mixture onto the base and sides of a 5-cm (2-in) deep, by 20-cm (8-in) square baking dish. Set aside.

To make the filling, beat cream cheese and mayonnaise until smooth. Mix in caster sugar, then eggs, one at a time. Add grated orange rind, lemon juice and vanilla and beat well. Turn into the prepared crust and bake according to instructions below, until just set. Cool on a wire rack, then chill. Serve topped with whipped cream and lemon or orange slices.

BROTHER
Hi-Speed at 200 °C for 10 minutes, then at 180 °C for 6-8 minutes.

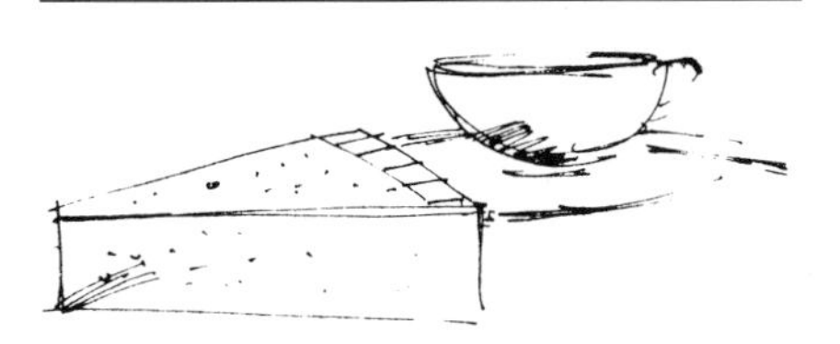

BANANA & BREAD CREAM

50%... 10 minutes
Serves 6

4 bananas
30 ml (2 tbsp) lemon juice
60 g (2 oz) sugar
5 slices high-protein white or wholemeal bread
butter
few drops of vanilla essence
60 ml (4 tbsp) dark rum
125 ml (4 fl oz) each cream and milk
2 eggs
generous pinch of mixed spice

Grease a soufflé dish well. Cut bananas into 1-cm (½-in) slices, toss in lemon juice and sugar. Trim crusts from the bread, butter generously, then cube. Place bananas and bread in soufflé dish. Beat vanilla, rum, cream, milk and eggs. Pour over bread and bananas. Sprinkle with mixed spice. Cover with vented plastic wrap and microwave on 50% for 8-10 minutes, until just set. Serve with hot rum sauce (page 92).

Strawberry & Cream Flan

STRAWBERRY & CREAM FLAN

Combination baking
Serves 10-12

175 g (6 oz) butter or margarine
175 g (6 oz) sugar
3 eggs
few drops of vanilla essence
175 g (6 oz) self-raising flour
pinch of salt
20-30 ml (4-6 tsp) hot water
FILLING
450 g (1 lb) strawberries
125 ml (4 fl oz) medium sherry
250 ml (8 fl oz) whipping cream
45 g ($1\frac{1}{2}$ oz) caster sugar

To make the flan, beat butter and sugar until light and fluffy. Add eggs, one at a time, beating well after each, then mix in vanilla. Sift flour with salt and fold into the egg mixture. Mix to a soft dropping consistency with the hot water.

Grease or spray a 30-cm (12-in) glass flan pan and line the centre with a circle of paper towel. Spread the flan mixture evenly in the prepared pan. Bake according to instructions below, in a preheated convection microwave oven until a skewer inserted in the centre comes out clean and the flan is lightly golden. Cool in the pan for about 10 minutes, then turn out and cool on a wire rack.

For the filling, hull and halve the berries and sprinkle with 90 ml (3 fl oz) of the sherry. Stand 20 minutes, then drain. Sprinkle the sherry over the cake. Whip the cream with the caster sugar to soft peaks. Add remaining sherry and beat to stiff peaks. Spread the cream in the centre of the flan. Arrange the berries on the cream and refrigerate until required.

BROTHER
Hi-Speed at 200 °C for 6-8 minutes.

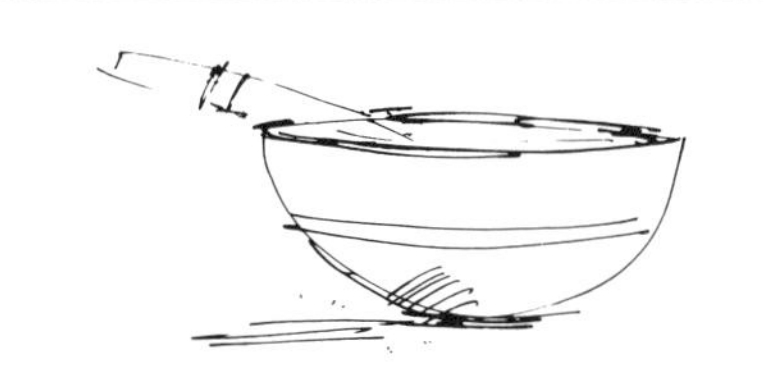

INDIVIDUAL STEAMED PUDDINGS

50%... 9 minutes
Serves 6

2 eggs
100 g ($3\frac{1}{2}$ oz) sugar
few drops of vanilla essence
250 ml (8 fl oz) milk
175 g (6 oz) self-raising flour
15 g ($\frac{1}{2}$ oz) margarine, melted
45 g ($1\frac{1}{2}$ oz) walnuts, chopped
treacle

Beat eggs and sugar together until pale. Add vanilla and milk and beat again. Sift the flour and add alternately with the milk, then beat in margarine. Grease 6 ramekins, sprinkle bases with nuts. Add about 15 ml (1 tbsp) treacle to each cup. Spoon mixture into cups, filling them just over half full. Cover with waxed paper. Microwave on 50% for 8-9 minutes. Stand for 5 minutes. Run a spatula around the edge of the cup, turn out. Serve with crème Anglaise (page 92) or custard.

THE ART OF BAKING

Front *Blueberry Lemon Cake*; back *Easy Soured Cream Chocolate Cake*

As with conventional baking, the use of good quality ingredients for microwave baking will ensure good results. Each ingredient has a specific purpose so it is important to read recipes carefully and to measure accurately.

YEAST BAKING

The microwave oven will prove yeast doughs and bake breads and rolls quickly and without effort. Breads baked by microwave energy alone will not brown or form the characteristic golden crust we have come to expect but combination baking, using convection and microwave energy, will give the traditional results.

YEAST is the raising agent in batters and doughs. This living organism is available in different forms. Compressed yeast comes in a cake and must be refrigerated. If it is purchased fresh, it will keep for about two weeks in the refrigerator or up to two months in the freezer. Dried yeast is available in granular form and will keep for several months if stored in a cool dry place. It requires a warmer liquid to activate it than compressed yeast. Instant dried yeast (sometimes called easy blend or fast action) also comes in granular form and can be used to shortcut the mixing and proving of yeast doughs. It is added to the dry ingredients and the warm liquid is mixed in, activating the yeast. Doughs using instant dried yeast prove much more quickly than those with ordinary dried yeast. It is important to follow the manufacturer's instructions as the method of using it varies with different brands. Remember that yeast is temperature sensitive; if the temperature of the liquid is too hot, the yeast action will be killed, and if the liquid is too cool, the growth will be retarded.

FLOUR is the major ingredient in bread. It contains a substance called gluten, which develops and helps to form the structural framework of each loaf when the dough is kneaded. Bread flour has a higher gluten content than ordinary plain flour and absorbs more liquid, giving a light texture and large volume. For most home-made yeast breads, however, plain flour can be used. A range of flour measurements is given in some yeast bread recipes as the changes in temperature and humidity affect the amount of flour needed. Wholemeal and rye flours add a distinctive flavour and texture to yeast breads and help to give a better colour to those that are baked in a microwave oven.

SUGAR provides food for the yeast, flavours the bread and gives a golden crust to the loaf.

SALT is used for flavour, but it also helps strengthen the structural framework of the bread.

BUTTER OR MARGARINE gives a tender rich bread and improves the browning. Because of the quick baking that takes place during microwave cooking, yeast doughs may need extra butter or margarine to prevent toughness and dryness. As a guideline when converting your own recipes for microwave baking, use about 60 g (2 oz) butter or margarine for every 350 g (12 oz) flour called for in the recipe.

LIQUID is an essential ingredient in yeast doughs. The warm liquid activates the yeast, thus starting the proving. Milk or water are the usual liquids in yeast doughs. When water is used in conventionally baked breads, the crust will be crisp and hard and the loaf will have an open texture. Milk gives a tender flavourful bread with a softer browner crust.

EGGS add richness and flavour to yeast mixtures, and their use results in a finer, more delicate texture.

OTHER INGREDIENTS Brown sugar and spices such as nutmeg or cinnamon do double duty in microwaved breads. They give special flavouring and add colour. This is particularly welcome in breads that are baked by microwave energy alone.

PREPARATION OF YEAST DOUGHS

MIXING The yeast needs to be well distributed throughout the dough and to make sure that this happens, thorough mixing is necessary. Yeast doughs can be mixed by hand, but many people prefer to use an electric mixer with a dough hook, or a food processor. A food processor will mix small amounts of bread quickly and efficiently while an electric mixer will handle large quantities. When using instant dried yeast, mix the yeast thoroughly with the dry ingredients before adding the warm liquid. Be sure that ingredients are at room temperature before mixing. If necessary, flour can be microwaved at 100% for 15-20 seconds before adding any other ingredients.

KNEADING After mixing in enough flour to form a good dough, the mixture must be kneaded to develop the gluten that forms the structure of the bread. A food processor or electric mixer will handle the task easily. If kneading dough by hand, turn the dough onto a lightly floured surface and sprinkle enough flour over the dough so that it will not stick to your hands. Stretch the dough by folding the edges over toward the centre, then press with your knuckles or heel of your hand. Repeat, giving the dough one quarter turn, until it is smooth and elastic and springs back into shape quickly when pressed with a finger.

PROVING THE DOUGH When the yeast dough rises, the yeast ferments and produces a gas, making the bread light in texture. Yeast dough can be put in a warm place to rise, but the microwave oven cuts down considerably on the time needed for proving.

To prove dough in the microwave oven, mix and knead the dough according to the recipe. Place dough in a large greased bowl and cover. Microwave on 100% for 15 seconds, then allow to rest in the microwave for 8-10 minutes. Repeat the process 2 or 3 times until the dough has doubled in size. Press your finger about 2.5 cm (1 in) into the dough – if the mark stays, the dough is well risen. The dough can then be knocked down and shaped as desired.

IMPROVING THE APPEARANCE OF MICROWAVED YEAST BREADS

As mentioned, yeast breads baked in the microwave do not brown. It is possible to improve the appearance and to give the appearance of a crust on these breads by adding a variety of ingredients to the top of the bread. Brush the top of the proven loaf with a little melted butter or margarine and sprinkle generously with one of the following: Crushed wheat, uncooked oatmeal, fine savoury biscuit crumbs, wheat germ, sesame or poppy seeds, a little yellow cornmeal, crushed seasoned cornflake crumbs, finely chopped nuts, crumbled potato crisps, dried herbs or, during the last few minutes of baking, a little grated cheese.

If you want the traditional appearance and finish on yeast breads, use the microwave oven to shortcut the preparation and proving time, then bake by combination or in a conventional oven.

REHEATING BREADS & ROLLS

It takes only 10-25 seconds to reheat one roll or slice of bread.

☐ To reheat, wrap the roll or bread in a paper towel or napkin and place in the microwave oven. Microwave on 100% for about 15 seconds, then check for warmness.

☐ For several rolls, place in a wicker basket and cover. Microwave for about 10 seconds per roll.

☐ Rolls or slices of bread containing sugar, icing or dried fruit will heat quickly, as the sugar attracts the microwaves.

QUICK BREADS

Quick breads include scones, griddle scones, tea breads, coffee cakes and other delicious bread mixtures that are made without yeast. These breads do not need time to prove. As these breads often include brown sugar, treacle, nuts, dried fruit or wholemeal flour, they are ideal for microwave baking as these ingredients give the finished breads an attractive appearance.

Quick breads use baking powder or bicarbonate of soda as a raising agent, but the other basic ingredients will be similar to yeast breads: sugar, flour, eggs, butter or margarine and liquid. Each bread will differ in the amounts used and in how they are mixed and baked.

Traditionally quick breads such as banana bread or nut bread are baked in loaves. There are microwave loaf pans available, but often the bread will bake more evenly in a ring pan.

SCONES can be baked by microwave energy, but will not brown in the conventional way unless baked with the aid of a browning dish or in a combination microwave oven.

AMERICAN MUFFINS do extremely well in the microwave oven and bake in just a few minutes. When converting your own muffin recipe to microwave baking, add 15-30 g (½-1 oz) more butter or margarine for every 125 g (4 oz) flour used.

FRUIT & NUT LOAVES are also baked successfully by microwave energy but it

is important to chop nuts and fruit finely as the batter thins out at the beginning of microwave cooking and large pieces of such ingredients may sink to the bottom of the pan.

TO TOAST SESAME SEEDS

Microwave a browning dish on 100% for 3 minutes. Sprinkle 45 ml (3 tbsp) sesame seeds onto dish. Cover with waxed paper, allow to stand for 2-3 minutes, stirring every 20 seconds.

HINTS FOR SUCCESSFUL QUICK BREADS

☐ Read the recipe before starting to work and assemble the ingredients. These mixtures should be combined quickly and baked immediately for best results.
☐ Measure accurately and mix the ingredients according to the recipe. Fill dishes or pans only half full as the mixture will rise high when baked in the microwave oven.
☐ For American muffins or scones, or other small individually baked items, arrange them in a circle on the turntable or microwave tray.
☐ American muffins will not have soggy bases if removed from the microwave muffin pan immediately after being taken out of the oven and allowed to stand on a wire rack to cool.
☐ To prepare baking pans for quick breads, grease or spray and line with waxed paper or paper towel. Do not flour the pan.
☐ Add brown sugar, treacle, spices, nuts and dried fruit or use wholemeal flour to make quick breads, scones and American muffins look more appealing.

PASTRY

Not all pastries are successful in the microwave oven but *shortcrust* and *suet* pastries become tender and flaky but do not brown when baked by microwave energy.

CRUMB CRUSTS can be baked quickly and easily in the microwave oven. Melt the butter or margarine directly in the pie plate, stir in the crumbs, sugar and other ingredients and press onto the base and sides of the plate. Biscuit crumbs have a good colour on their own and need no additional colour. Microwave the crumb crust for about 1½ minutes, or as directed in each recipe. Use fillings that require little or no cooking.

CHOUX PASTRY can be made in the microwave oven but like *puff* pastry needs hot dry air to give it its characteristic crispy brown finish and, therefore, is not suitable for baking by microwave energy alone.

HINTS FOR MICROWAVED PASTRY

☐ Brush the uncooked pastry shell with a little egg yolk or vanilla essence mixed with water, or add a few drops of yellow food colouring to the dough to improve the colour.
☐ For fine shortcrust pastry, keep the ingredients cool and handle very lightly. Butter or margarine should be rubbed into the flour while still chilled. The rubbing in can be done by hand, or with an electric mixer or food processor, but take care not to overmix.
☐ The egg and liquid should be added quickly and with caution so that only enough is added to bind the mixture together. Too much liquid results in a sticky pastry that is difficult to handle.
☐ After mixing, roll the pastry gently into shape on a lightly floured surface. Avoid turning the pastry over during rolling, and avoid stretching the pastry as it will shrink back into shape during baking. Lift the dough carefully, perhaps by folding it over a rolling pin, and fit it into the pie plate or flan dish.
☐ Before adding a moist or juicy filling that requires baking, seal the pastry by brushing it with beaten egg yolk.
☐ Single crust pies are best for microwave baking, as a double crust pie does not cook properly and the bottom tends to become soggy.

TO MICROWAVE SHORTCRUST PASTRY SHELLS

Most microwaved pies use a pre-baked shell. If the shell is not at least partially baked before adding a filling, it absorbs moisture and becomes soggy.

Line the pie plate with pastry and trim edges. Cut a long aluminium foil strip about 2.5-cm (1-in) wide and cover the edges of the pastry shell to keep it from becoming overcooked. Prick the pastry with a fork if it is to be used with a chilled filling. Place a double thickness of paper towel in the base of the shell, pressing gently into the edges. Microwave on 100% for 3-4 minutes, remove the foil and paper towel and microwave for 1½-2 minutes more if necessary. Cool the crust before using.

TO BAKE LARGE TARTS & PIES

BROTHER
Hi-Speed at 250 °C for 14 minutes.

TO BAKE SMALL TARTLETS & SAUSAGE ROLLS

BROTHER
Hi-Speed at 250 °C for 5 minutes, then on Turbo for a further 5 minutes.

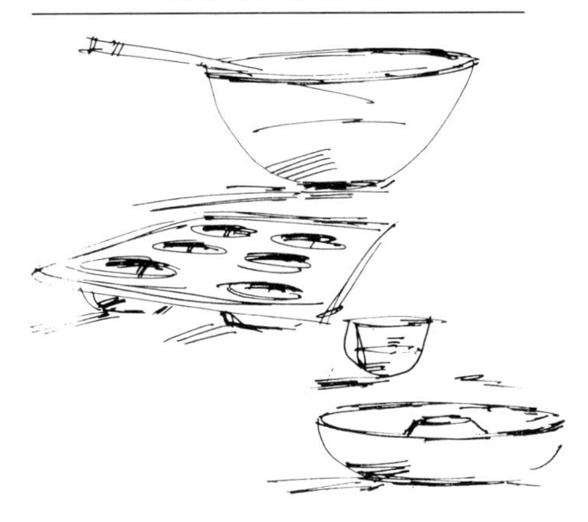

TART CRUST

100%... 3½ minutes
Makes 1 × 20-23-cm (8-9-in) pie shell

125 g (4 oz) plain flour
100 g (3½ oz) caster sugar
generous pinch of cinnamon
generous pinch of salt
60 g (2 oz) margarine
1 egg
few drops of egg yellow food colouring
extra flour

Sift flour, sugar, cinnamon and salt, rub in margarine. Lightly beat egg and colouring, add to flour and mix or process to form a ball. Add a little extra flour if the mixture is too soft to roll out. Wrap in foil and refrigerate for 30 minutes. Roll out to fit a 20-23-cm (8-9-in) pie plate. Cut a piece of waxed paper large enough to fill the middle and go up the sides of the dish, add a layer of beans or rice. Microwave on 100% for 3-3½ minutes. Cool before adding filling.

BASIC CRUMB CRUST

100%...2½ minutes
Makes 1 × 23-cm (9-in) pie shell

60 g (2 oz) butter
100 g (3½ oz) Marie, or digestive biscuit crumbs
30 g (1 oz) soft brown sugar
pinch of cinnamon

Microwave butter in a 23-cm (9-in) pie plate on 100% for 45-60 seconds. Add crumbs, brown sugar and cinnamon and mix well. Gently press the mixture onto the bottom and sides of the plate. Microwave on 100% for 1-1½ minutes. Cool before adding a filling.

VARIATIONS

Nutty crust Proceed as for basic crust, adding 45 g (1½ oz) chopped nuts and 30 ml (2 tbsp) single cream to the mixture.

Spicy crust Use 100 g (3½ oz) ginger biscuit crumbs. Substitute 2.5 ml (½ tsp) mixed spice for the cinnamon and add 30 ml (2 tbsp) single cream.

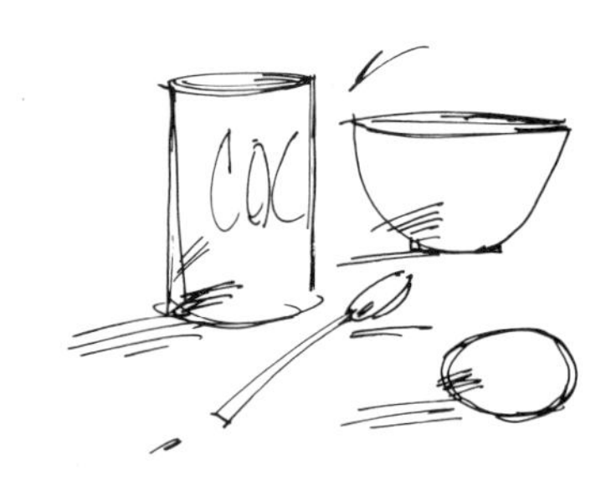

CHOCOLATE CRUMB CRUST

100%...2½ minutes
Makes 1 × 23-cm (9-in) pie shell

10-12 chocolate digestive or chocolate cream biscuits, broken
60 g (2 oz) butter
30 ml (2 tbsp) single cream

Place biscuits in a food processor with a metal blade and process to fine crumbs. Microwave butter in a 23-cm (9-in) pie plate on 100% for 45-60 seconds. Add crumbs and cream and mix well. Press onto the base and sides of the dish and microwave on 100% for 1-1½ minutes. Cool before using.

WHOLEMEAL PASTRY

Makes 1 × 23-25-cm (9-10-in) single pie crust

200 g (7 oz) wholemeal flour
7.5 ml (1½ tsp) baking powder
2.5 ml (½ tsp) salt
125 g (4 oz) butter or margarine, cubed
1 egg yolk
iced water

Place the dry ingredients in the work bowl of a food processor or mixer. Add butter and rub in. Combine the yolk and a little water, add to the dry ingredients and work to form a firm dough. Rest pastry for 15 minutes. Roll out and use as required.

MUESLI PIE CRUST

100%...4 minutes
Makes 1 × 23-cm (9-in) pie shell

100 g (3½ oz) biscuit crumbs
45 g (1½ oz) muesli
5 ml (1 tsp) cinnamon
30 ml (2 tbsp) ground almonds
100 g (3½ oz) butter
45 ml (3 tbsp) single cream

Mix biscuit crumbs, muesli, cinnamon and almonds together. Microwave butter on 100% for 1½-2 minutes to melt. Add to dry ingredients, mixing well. Add cream and mix in. Press onto base and sides of a 23-cm (9-in) pie plate and microwave for 2 minutes. Allow to cool before using.

QUICK PUFF PASTRY

Makes 250 g (9 oz)

250 g (9 oz) plain flour
2.5 ml (½ tsp) salt
5 ml (1 tsp) cream of tartar
200 g (7 oz) cold butter, grated and re-chilled
about 185 ml (6 fl oz) cold soda water
15 ml (1 tbsp) brandy

Sift the flour, salt and cream of tartar into a bowl. Add cold butter and toss lightly with a metal spatula to coat the butter with flour. Combine soda water and brandy and add at least three-quarters of the liquid to the flour mixture. Combine with metal spatula, adding sufficient liquid to form a firm dough. Wrap pastry in foil and refrigerate for 15 minutes. Turn dough onto a lightly floured board. Roll into a rectangular shape. Dust very lightly with flour and fold into three. Give the pastry a quarter turn so that the fold is now to one side. Seal edges lightly using the rolling pin. Repeat the rolling, folding and sealing. Rest in the refrigerator for 20 minutes, then repeat the two rollings and foldings and resting period twice more, giving 6 rolling and folding processes. Allow pastry to rest for 20 minutes before using as required.

CHOUX PASTRY

100%...3 minutes
plus Convection baking

150 ml (5 fl oz) water
scant 45 g (1½ oz) margarine
pinch of salt
60 g (2 oz) plain flour, sifted
2 eggs
few drops of vanilla essence (for sweet choux)

Place water, margarine and salt in a large jug, microwave on 100% for 2 minutes, stir. Add flour and mix well. Microwave for 1 minute, beating well after 30 seconds. Allow to cool. Beat eggs and vanilla, add half the egg mixture to the flour mixture and beat well with an electric mixer. Add remaining egg gradually, beating well after each addition. If the mixture starts to lose shape do not add any more egg. Beat for at least one minute. Pipe or spoon shapes onto a greased baking sheet.

Bake on convection at 200 °C (400 °F) for 25 minutes. Remove from the oven, immediately make a hole on the underside of the pastry to allow the steam to escape. Cool on a wire rack and use as required.

SHORTCRUST PASTRY

100%...6 minutes
Makes 1 × 20-23-cm (8-9-in) single pie shell

125 g (4 oz) plain flour
2.5 ml (½ tsp) salt
5 ml (1 tsp) sugar
60 g (2 oz) butter
1 egg yolk
45 ml (3 tbsp) cold water

Combine flour, salt and sugar. Rub in butter until mixture resembles fine crumbs. Combine egg yolk and water and add enough to the dry ingredients to form a dough. Turn pastry onto a lightly floured surface and knead gently, then roll out and use as desired.

To microwave pastry shells, line pie plate with pastry. Cut a long foil strip about 2.5-cm (1-in) wide and line the edge of the pastry shell. Place a double layer of paper towel in the base of the pastry shell, pressing gently into the edges. Microwave on 100% for 3½-4 minutes. Remove foil and paper towel and microwave for 1½-2 minutes more. Use cooked pastry shells for pies and tarts with cold or uncooked fillings.

VARIATIONS

Herb pastry Omit sugar and add 5 ml (1 tsp) herbs of your choice.
Cheese pastry Omit sugar, add large pinch of dry mustard to the dry ingredients and stir in 45 ml (3 tbsp) grated cheese after rubbing in the butter.
Sweet pastry Increase the sugar to 45 g (1½ oz), add few drops of vanilla essence, and proceed as for shortcrust pastry.

CAKES

It is important to understand the function of all the ingredients in the cake mixture.

FLOUR All the cakes in this book have been tested with the type of flour specified in the recipe. Do not substitute types of flour as the success of each cake depends on the use of specific ingredients. If the recipe calls for sifted flour, be sure to follow instructions as the sifting aerates the flour and gives a better texture to the cake.

BUTTER & MARGARINE Butter gives a good flavour to cakes but margarine may be substituted. White vegetable fats do not contain much flavour but may be combined with butter or margarine for baking. Some cakes may call for oil, and if so, measure accurately. When adapting your own recipes, you may wish to increase the butter or margarine by about 30 g (1 oz) for every 125 g (4 oz) flour.

SUGAR In recipes calling for 'sugar', granulated sugar is used. Caster sugar is used in recipes for light cakes with a fine texture. Brown sugar gives added colour and a good flavour.

EGGS help to form the structure of cakes and give them a light texture. When converting your own recipes to microwave baking, you may wish to add an extra egg to the mixture to increase the firmness of the texture.

RAISING AGENT Baking powder is used as the raising agent in many cakes. It is usually sifted with the dry ingredients and when moistened it releases a gas that causes the cake to rise. Bicarbonate of soda may be used when an acid liquid, such as soured milk, buttermilk or yoghurt, is added to a cake.

LIQUIDS Milk, water, buttermilk, soured cream, yoghurt and some fruit juices are all liquids that can be used in baking. Each will give its characteristic flavour to the cake. Be sure to measure accurately.

OTHER INGREDIENTS such as nuts, spices, fruit and dried fruit add delicious flavour and some colour to cakes and should be used in the quantities specified. In the case of fruit, dried fruit and candied peel, do not increase the quantities as this may cause burned spots in the cake.

MIXING CAKE BATTERS

There are two basic methods for mixing cake batters. It is important to follow directions for mixing exactly to ensure the success of the cake.

CREAMING In this methods, the butter or margarine, sugar and eggs are mixed together until light and fluffy, then the dry ingredients and liquid are added alternately and blended until smooth. Most of the old-fashioned or standard cake recipes call for this method of mixing. It is important not to overmix the batter for microwave cakes.

QUICK MIXING The butter or margarine, dry ingredients and part of the liquid are mixed, then the remaining liquid and eggs are added. This method takes less time than the creaming method and works well for some cakes. Take care not to overmix.

PREPARATION OF BAKING PANS

Pan preparation differs from that of conventional baking. Pans can be greased or sprayed, but must not be floured. The flour will bake on the outside of the cake, causing a sticky, soggy surface. If the cake is not to be iced, the bottom and sides of the pan can be sprinkled with finely chopped nuts or fine sweet biscuit crumbs. For cakes that are to be turned out and iced, grease the pan, then line the bottom with a circle of waxed paper or white paper towel.

Preparation of pans for combination baking is very similar to that of conventional baking. Grease, flour and line pans before adding the cake mixture.

NOTE Follow the instructions given for your Combination oven regarding which containers to use and placement of pans and racks.

TESTING IF COOKED

Always test if cake is cooked at the minimum time given in each recipe. It is easy to add seconds to the baking time, but overcooking toughens baked goods. Cakes should spring back when lightly pressed in the centre. If there are moist spots, touch them with your finger. The top should come off on your finger, but the cake underneath should look dry. Moist spots will evaporate during the standing time. If the cake is still doughy underneath the spots, the cake will require some additional baking time. With glass containers, you can check the bottom of the cake too. If there seems to be a large uncooked area in the centre, shield the edges with aluminium foil and continue microwaving for a short period.

Another test is to insert a skewer near the centre of the cake. If the skewer comes out almost clean the cake is cooked. If you have trouble with doughy centres on round cakes, you may have to elevate the dish by placing it on a microwave rack. This gives the microwaves a better chance to penetrate evenly from the bottom as well as the top of the cake.

STANDING TIME

Cakes continue to cook after being removed from the microwave oven, so it is necessary to let them 'stand' before turning out to cool. Cakes should be placed on a heatproof surface, such as a counter or wooden board during standing time, not on a wire cooling rack. Allow to stand for the time suggested in each recipe, usually 5-15 minutes, then turn out onto a wire rack to cool. Handle the cake gently when turning out to cool. Loosen edges before inverting. Always cool cakes right side up unless otherwise directed and always cool completely before icing.

CONVERTING RECIPES

The best recipes for microwave baking are those in rich in butter or margarine and eggs. If the recipe you want to convert is not rich, add an extra egg and about 30 g (1 oz) butter or margarine to the mixture. If the recipe contains 3 or more eggs, you may wish to decrease the liquid called for by about a quarter. Be sure to select the correct pan sizes, but the pans will need to be deeper than for conventional baking. For microwave baking, check if ready at one quarter of the conventional time, and add more time if necessary.

HINTS FOR MICROWAVED CAKES

☐ Always read the recipe carefully before starting to work so that you understand each step.

☐ Collect and measure ingredients before starting to mix the batter.

☐ Measure correctly, don't guess. Use standard metric utensils. The success of each recipe depends on the accurate combination of ingredients.

☐ Remove large air bubbles from the batter before baking by tapping the pan lightly on the work surface, or by cutting gently through the batter with a knife.

☐ Do not overmix, especially with the creamed mixture. Too much air in the mixture will cause the cake to rise during baking, but it may settle during cooling and give the cake an unattractive appearance.

☐ Avoid overbaking. Always check for doneness at the minimum time, adding more time if necessary. Remember you can check the progress of the cake often: unlike conventional baking, the cake will not flop if the door is opened briefly.

☐ The centre of a heavy or very rich cake, such as a carrot or fruit cake, may be hollowed out slightly before baking to prevent doming or cracking of the finished cake.

☐ Be sure to use the pan size given in each recipe.

☐ If moisture on cakes does not firm up during the standing time, try covering the cake loosely with waxed paper to keep in some of the heat.

☐ If your microwave does not have a turntable, you may find that rotating the baking pan occasionally during baking will prevent it baking unevenly.

☐ With many cakes, the batter can be left to stand for 3-4 minutes before microwaving in order to start the reaction of the raising agent and liquid. This will result in better volume.

☐ Many microwaved cakes are best eaten on the day they are baked. They are so quick and easy to make that it is possible to make them just minutes before serving.

☐ Because cakes rise higher when baked in a microwave oven, fill dishes only half full. If your microwave containers are not deep enough to handle the entire mixture, bake a few cup cakes with the remaining mixture.

☐ To make a ring pan for microwave baking, place a glass tumbler, open side up, in the centre of a deep, round ovenproof dish. Hold the glass in place while filling the dish. Remember to grease the tumbler as well as the dish before adding the cake mixture.

CAKE MIXES

Pre-prepared cake mixes bake very well in the microwave oven, and many manufacturers include microwave instructions on the packet. If no microwave directions are given, mix as directed on the packet adding an extra egg if desired. Turn mixture into a prepared ring pan and place on a rack in the microwave oven. Microwave on 30% for 6 minutes, then on 100% for about 4 minutes, or until the surface is almost dry. Alternately, microwave on 100% for 6 minutes, then check if cake is cooked and add extra time if necessary.

CAKES & QUICK FRUIT CAKE MIXTURES

These bake more evenly in round containers, but can be baked in square containers with the corners shielded. Pans containing mixtures that are heavy and moist should be elevated during baking to ensure even baking.

FREEZING CAKES

Many cakes can be frozen. If the cake is filled or iced, freeze before wrapping. Plain cakes can be wrapped before freezing. Be sure cakes are completely cool before wrapping and freezing.

DEFROSTING CAKES

The defrosting of cakes and baked goods is started by the microwave energy, while the standing time finishes the process.

DEFROSTING CHART

		Defrost (30%)	Standing Time	
BREAD				
Bread, whole or sliced	1 kg (2¼ lb)	6-8 minutes	5 minutes	Unwrap. Place on paper towel. Turn over during defrosting.
Bread	25×12-cm (10×5-in)	4-6 minutes	5 minutes	Unwrap. Place on paper towel. Turn over during defrosting.
Bread	1 slice	10-15 seconds	1-2 minutes	Unwrap. Place on paper towel. Time accurately.
Bread rolls	2 4	20-25 seconds 30-40 seconds	1-2 minutes 1-2 minutes	Unwrap. Place on paper towel.
CAKES				
Cup cakes or American muffins	4	1-1½ minutes	5 minutes	Unwrap. Place on paper towel.
Sponge cake	23-cm (9-in)	2-3 minutes	5 minutes	Unwrap. Place on paper towel. Turn over after 1 minute.
Doughnuts or sweet buns	4	1½-2 minutes	5 minutes	Unwrap. Place on paper towel. Turn over after 1 minute.
Loaf cakes or ring cakes	25×12-cm or 23-25-cm (10×5-in or 9-10-in)	5-7 minutes	10 minutes	Unwrap. Place on paper towel. Turn over after 3 minutes.
Bars	20-23-cm (8-9-in) square	4-6 minutes	5-10 minutes	Unwrap. Place on paper towel.
Pancakes or crêpes	10	3-4 minutes	–	Unwrap. Place on plate. Cover with plastic wrap.
PIES				
Pies or tarts	20-23-cm (8-9-in)	4-6 minutes	10 minutes	Unwrap.
Individual pies	1 small 4 small	25-30 seconds 2-3 minutes	2 minutes 2 minutes	Unwrap. Place upside down on paper towel.

BISCUITS

When using the microwave oven for biscuits, note that those with crumbly, stiff batters will give good results. Remember that only a few biscuits can be baked at one time, so large batches will take longer to microwave than to bake conventionally. The texture and colour of microwaved biscuits differ somewhat from those baked conventionally, so select recipes for biscuits that have good natural colour, or that will be iced. A combination microwave oven will give good results but once again, the number of biscuits baked at one time is limited.

BARS & SQUARES

Bars microwave very successfully, but they need to be iced, dusted with icing sugar or topped with nuts or melted chocolate to give them a more attractive appearance. Bars are typically baked in square pans but remember to shield the corners with aluminium foil to prevent over-baking (page 9).

CUP CAKES

Cup cakes or fairy cakes microwave very quickly and need close attention. Be sure to fill cups no more than half full and when baking more than two at a time, arrange them in a circle on the turntable or microwave tray. As a general guide, microwave cup cakes or fairy cakes as follows:

Number	Time on 100%
1	20-30 seconds
2	45-60 seconds
3	1 to 1 minute 15 seconds
4	1 minute 20 seconds to 1 minute 30 seconds
5	2 minutes to 2 minutes 15 seconds
6	2 minutes 30 seconds to 2 minutes 45 seconds

CREAMY ICING

100%... 3 minutes
Fills and ices 1 × 20-cm (8-in) cake

300 ml (10 fl oz) milk
30 g (1 oz) cornflour
175 g (6 oz) butter or margarine
175 g (6 oz) caster sugar
few drops of vanilla essence

Microwave 280 ml (9 fl oz) of the milk on 100% for 2 minutes. Combine remaining milk with cornflour, pour on boiling milk and stir well. Microwave for 1 minute until very thick, then beat well. Cool until just warm. Meanwhile cream butter and sugar well, add vanilla. Beat in cornflour mixture about a quarter at a time, beating very well. Use for filling and icing sponge-type cakes or puff pastry layers.

ORANGE GLAZE

Ices 1 ring cake

150 g (5 oz) icing sugar
5 ml (1 tsp) grated orange rind
20 ml (4 tsp) orange juice
15 g (½ oz) butter or margarine

Beat all ingredients until smooth and use to glaze cakes.

CHOCOLATE ICING

50%... 2 minutes
Ices 2 × 23-cm (9-in) layers or 24 biscuits

60 g (2 oz) plain chocolate, chopped
45 g (1½ oz) butter
200 g (7 oz) icing sugar, sifted
pinch of salt
1 egg
185 ml (6 fl oz) single cream
few drops of vanilla essence

Place chocolate and butter in a jug and microwave on 50% for about 2 minutes, until just melted, stirring after 1 minute. Turn into a large bowl and beat in the icing sugar, salt and egg. Beat until smooth. Chill mixture well, then beat in cream and vanilla and continue to beat for 3-4 minutes until thick. Chill until required.

CHOCOLATE POURING ICING

100%... 2 minutes
Ices 1 × 20-cm (8-in) cake

This icing forms a lovely smooth top for any sponge cake and makes an excellent topping for eclairs.

250 g (9 oz) icing sugar, sifted
45 ml (3 tbsp) cocoa powder
10 ml (2 tsp) instant coffee granules
30 ml (2 tbsp) milk
15 g (½ oz) margarine

Place all the ingredients in a bowl. Microwave on 100% for 2 minutes, until bubbling. Stir well, then pour over the cake and eclairs.

CHOCOLATE ORANGE ICING

Ices 1 × 20-cm (8-in) cake

200 g (7 oz) icing sugar
30 ml (2 tbsp) cocoa powder
15 g (½ oz) soft butter
30 ml (2 tbsp) orange juice
45 ml (3 tbsp) chopped pecan nuts (optional)

Sift the icing sugar and cocoa powder into a bowl, mix in the butter and enough orange juice to form a stiff paste, then beat over hot water until smooth and spreadable. Use to ice chocolate orange pecan cake (page 53) and sprinkle with pecans if desired.

CHOCOLATE COATING ICING

100%... 3 minutes
Makes about 200 ml (6½ fl oz)

45 g (1½ oz) sugar
45 ml (3 tbsp) water
45 g (1½ oz) plain chocolate, chopped
30 ml (2 tbsp) cocoa powder
45 g (1½ oz) butter

Combine all the ingredients except the butter in a bowl. Microwave on 100% for 2-3 minutes, stirring every 30 seconds, the sugar must be dissolved. Beat well, then beat in butter. Continue beating until the mixture begins to leave a trail. Use as a topping for layer cakes or choux pastries.

BANANA FUDGE ICING

70%, 50%…8 minutes
Ices 1 × 25-cm (10-in) ring or
1 × 20-cm (8-in) single cake

30 g (1 oz) butter
175 g (6 oz) soft brown sugar
45 ml (3 tbsp) milk
150 g (5 oz) icing sugar, sifted
15 ml (1 tbsp) single cream
1 banana, sliced
lemon juice

Place butter, brown sugar and milk in a bowl. Microwave on 50% for 5 minutes. Stir well. Microwave on 70% for 3 minutes. Pour into a cold bowl and cool slightly. Beat in icing sugar and cream. The mixture should have a 'drizzling' consistency. Use this icing to sandwich 2 cake layers together or drizzle over a ring cake. Whilst still soft, decorate icing with slices of banana, which have been dipped in lemon juice.

FLUFFY ICING

100%…6 minutes
Ices 1 × 20-cm (8-in) square cake

100 g (3½ oz) sugar
40 ml (8 tsp) water
pinch of cream of tartar
pinch of salt
1 egg white
few drops of vanilla essence

Combine sugar, water, cream of tartar and salt in a large jug or deep casserole. Microwave on 100% for 2 minutes. Stir well. Microwave for 2-4 minutes longer, or until a soft ball forms when a small amount is dropped in cold water. Beat egg white until stiff. Slowly pour in hot syrup, beating constantly, until mixture is stiff and glossy. Add vanilla during the final beating.

COFFEE BUTTERCREAM

100%, 50%…4 minutes
Fills and ices 1 × 23-cm
(9-in) layer cake

125 ml (4 fl oz) single cream
60 g (2 oz) caster sugar
5 ml (1 tsp) powdered gelatine
60 ml (4 tbsp) strong hot black coffee
5 ml (1 tsp) instant coffee granules
2 egg yolks
250 g (9 oz) soft butter
250 g (9 oz) icing sugar, sifted
few drops of vanilla essence

Place the cream, caster sugar, gelatine, coffee and coffee granules in a jug. Microwave on 100% for 2 minutes. Beat egg yolks well and beat in hot liquid. Microwave on 50% for 2 minutes, stirring every 30 seconds. Allow to cool. Cream butter well, gradually beat in icing sugar and then the vanilla. Slowly beat in coffee custard, beating until smooth. Chill for 30 minutes before using.

CREAM CHEESE ICING

30%... 1 minute
Ices 1 × 25-cm (10-in) ring cake

60 g (2 oz) butter
125 g (4 oz) cream cheese
125 g (4 oz) caster sugar
125 g (4 oz) icing sugar
10 ml (2 tsp) lemon juice or
few drops of vanilla essence

Soften butter in the microwave on 30% for about 1 minute if necessary. Using an electric mixer beat butter and cream cheese together. Slowly add sugars, then lemon juice or vanilla, beating well after each addition. Use as required.

BROWNED BUTTER ICING

100%... 4 minutes
Ices 18 cup cakes or 1 × 20-cm (8-in) sponge

60 g (2 oz) butter
250 g (9 oz) icing sugar, sifted
few drops of vanilla essence

Place butter in a jug, microwave on 100% for 3-4 minutes, until brown. Mix in the icing sugar and then the vanilla.

CHOCOLATE FUDGE ICING

70%... 2 minutes
Ices 1 × 20-cm (8-in) cake

125 g (4 oz) icing sugar, sifted
few drops of vanilla essence
30 ml (2 tbsp) cocoa powder
15 g (½ oz) margarine
30 ml (2 tbsp) milk

Place all the ingredients in a large jug, stir. Microwave on 70% for 2 minutes. Stir well and pour over the cake.

COCONUT CREAM

100%... 3 minutes
Makes about 400 ml (13 fl oz)

200 g (7 oz) desiccated coconut,
or fresh coconut, grated
375 ml (12 fl oz) water
125 ml (4 fl oz) single cream

Place coconut in the work bowl of a food processor, fitted with a metal blade. Combine water and cream in a 1-litre (1¾-pint) jug. Microwave on 100% for 3-4 minutes until just boiling. With the machine running, slowly add boiling liquid to the coconut. Process for 1 minute, then allow mixture to cool for 5 minutes. Strain through a sieve lined with a double layer of butter muslin. Press the coconut with a wooden spoon to extract the liquid. Now bring the corners of the cloth together and squeeze out any remaining liquid. Keep the liquid covered in the refrigerator and use as required.

HUNGARIAN ICING

70%... 3 minutes
Ices 1 × 20-cm (8-in) layer cake

100 g (3½ oz) milk chocolate, chopped
30 ml (2 tbsp) water
250 g (9 oz) icing sugar, sifted
3 egg yolks
45 g (1½ oz) soft butter
nuts

Place chocolate and water in a large bowl, microwave on 70% for about 3 minutes, stirring every minute. Beat in icing sugar and yolks, beat in icing sugar and yolks, beat very well. Lastly beat in butter. Use to fill and top a 20-cm (8-in) layer cake, then sprinkle with chopped nuts. (If the icing is a little too soft, refrigerate for about 30 minutes.)

LEMON FILLING FOR CHOUX PASTRY

100%, 50%... 6 minutes
Makes about 600 ml (1 pint)

200 g (7 oz) sugar
30 g (1 oz) cornflour
pinch of salt
375 ml (12 fl oz) water
3 egg yolks, beaten
75 ml (2½ fl oz) lemon juice
60 g (2 oz) butter

Combine sugar, cornflour and salt in a bowl. Stir in water. Microwave on 100% for 4 minutes, stirring every 30 seconds. Stir a little of the hot mixture into egg

yolks, then pour yolks into bowl containing hot mixture. Microwave on 50% for 2 minutes, stirring every 30 seconds. Stir in lemon juice and butter. Cover with waxed paper, then cool and chill. Use to fill choux puffs.

RUM & ORANGE SAUCE

100%... 3 minutes
Makes about 250 ml (8 fl oz)

Delicious with Christmas pudding.

150 ml (5 fl oz) orange juice
30 ml (2 tbsp) lemon juice
grated rind of 1 orange
5 ml (1 tsp) cornflour
30 ml (2 tbsp) golden syrup
30 ml (2 tbsp) soft brown sugar
15-30 ml (1-2 tbsp) dark rum

Combine orange juice, lemon juice, and orange rind. Blend a little of the liquid into the cornflour, then stir into the remaining liquid. Mix in golden syrup, brown sugar and rum. Microwave, covered, on 100% for 3 minutes, stirring every 30 seconds.

CRÈME ANGLAISE

100%... 5 minutes
Makes about 300 ml (10 fl oz)

2 egg yolks
15 g (½ oz) plain flour
15 g (½ oz) cornflour
30 g (1 oz) sugar
300 ml (10 fl oz) milk
few drops of vanilla essence

Place yolks, flour, cornflour, sugar and a little milk into a bowl, beat to a smooth cream. Microwave the remaining milk on 100% for 2-3 minutes, until just boiling. Pour a little of the hot milk onto creamed mixture, stir well. Add remaining milk and vanilla, microwave for 1-2 minutes, whisking every 30 seconds. Serve hot or cold. To cool, cover sauce directly with greaseproof paper. This will prevent a skin from forming.

CARAMEL SYRUP

100%...8 minutes
Makes about 200 ml (7 fl oz)

150 g (5 oz) sugar
100 ml (3½ fl oz) water

Mix sugar and water together in a medium-sized bowl. Microwave on 100% for 2 minutes. Stir and brush the sides of the bowl with a little water to remove sugar crystals. Microwave for a further 6-8 minutes, until a good deep caramel colour forms.

RUM SAUCE

100%...4 minutes
Makes about 300 ml (10 fl oz)

125 ml (4 fl oz) water
125 g (4 oz) caster sugar
60 ml (4 tbsp) dark rum

Combine water and sugar in a large jug. Microwave on 100% for 4 minutes, stirring every minute. Cool slightly, then stir in the rum. Reheat when required.

CITRUS SAUCE

100%...4 minutes
Makes about 300 ml (10 fl oz)

A delicious sauce to serve with pound cake or gingerbread.

100 g (3½ oz) sugar
20 ml (4 tsp) cornflour
2.5 ml (½ tsp) cinnamon
250 ml (8 fl oz) hot water
15 ml (1 tbsp) lemon juice or orange juice
15 ml (1 tbsp) grated lemon or orange rind
30 g (1 oz) butter

Combine sugar, cornflour, cinnamon and water in a large jug. Add lemon or orange juice and rind. Cover and microwave on 100% for 4 minutes, stirring after 2 minutes. Stir in butter and serve warm.

TOMATO TOPPING

100%...20 minutes
Makes about 500 ml (16 fl oz)

800 g (1 lb 14 oz) canned tomatoes
15 ml (1 tbsp) oil
salt and black pepper
5 ml (1 tsp) sugar
1-2 garlic cloves, crushed
15 ml (1 tbsp) chopped fresh basil or 5 ml (1 tsp) dried

Drain tomato liquid into a large bowl, cut tomatoes up roughly and add to juice. Add oil, salt, pepper and sugar. Microwave on 100% for 20 minutes, stirring every 5 minutes. When thickened, add garlic and basil.

BASIC CRÊPE MIXTURE

Makes about 20 crêpes

125 g (4 oz) plain flour
generous pinch of salt
2 eggs
150 ml (5 fl oz) milk
150 ml (5 fl oz) water
30 ml (2 tbsp) oil

To make the batter, place all the ingredients into a blender or processor. Blend for 30 seconds, scrape down the goblet and process for a further 30 seconds. Stand for 30 minutes before using. If crêpes rather than pancakes are required, thin down the batter – the thinner the batter, the thinner the crêpe. Heat a crêpe pan until a slight haze forms. Wipe the pan with a little oil. Spoon sufficient mixture into the pan to coat the base thinly. Cook for a few seconds. Carefully loosen the edges with a spatula, turn crêpe over and cook for a few seconds. Lift out of the pan onto a sheet of greaseproof paper.

WHOLEMEAL CRÊPES

Makes about 20 crêpes

125 g (4 oz) wholemeal flour
2.5 ml (½ tsp) salt
1 egg, beaten
300 ml (10 fl oz) milk
15 ml (1 tbsp) oil

Combine flour and salt, beat in the egg, milk and oil to make a smooth batter. Allow to stand for 30 minutes. Heat a heavy frying pan and wipe with oil. Spoon in enough batter to coat the base of the pan and cook until bubbles appear. Turn the crêpes over and cook the other side until golden. Cool, then use as desired.

MICROWAVE HOT WATER SPONGE

100%...6 minutes
Makes 1 × 20-cm (8-in), deep cake

125 g (4 oz) plain flour
30 g (1 oz) cornflour
generous pinch of salt
10 ml (2 tsp) baking powder
3 eggs, separated
60 ml (4 tbsp) oil
125 ml (4 fl oz) hot water
175 g (6 oz) sugar
few drops of vanilla essence or almond essence

Grease or spray a deep 20-cm (8-in) microwave baking dish, line the base with plastic wrap or greaseproof paper. Sift together the flour, cornflour, salt and baking powder, set aside. Beat yolks, oil, hot water, sugar and vanilla together very well. Add flour mixture and beat to combine. Beat egg whites until soft peaks form, fold into cake mixture. Turn into prepared dish and microwave on 100% for 5-6 minutes. Allow cake to cool on a flat surface for 10 minutes before turning out onto a wire rack. Peel off plastic wrap or greaseproof paper. Use as required.

TOASTED BREADCRUMBS

100%...7 minutes

250 ml (60 g) fresh white or brown breadcrumbs

Preheat a browning dish on 100% for 3-4 minutes. Spread breadcrumbs on heated dish. Stir for about 30 seconds. Microwave for 2-3 minutes more until golden brown, stirring every 30 seconds. Allow to cool before storing.